Praise for Becoming a Prayer Warrior

Beth Alves has a beautiful way of expressing deep truths with simplicity and clarity. *Becoming a Prayer Warrior* has blessed my life, and you, too, will receive blessing and insight through the pages of this book.

Bobbye Byerly
Director of Prayer, World Prayer Center
Colorado Springs, Colorado

"Been there, done that" is a popular slogan these days. When it comes to in-depth intercession and practical patterns for personal prayer, *Becoming a Prayer Warrior* will take you where Beth Alves has "been" so you can do "that," too!

Dick Eastman
International President, Every Home for Christ
Colorado Springs, Colorado

Are you a believer who longs to deepen your prayer life—yet you struggle with feeling guilty and inadequate? *Becoming a Prayer Warrior* will increase your understanding of prayer and provide practical guidelines to help you become an effective prayer warrior.

Ruthanne Garlock
Coauthor, How to Pray for Your Children
Bulverde, Texas

Beth Alves is a woman of prayer! She has taught the principles of prayer found in *Becoming a Prayer Warrior* at Cornerstone Church, producing a blessed time of brokenness and spiritual refreshing. I recommend her book to you.

John Hagee
Senior Pastor, Cornerstone Church
San Antonio, Texas

D0972498

As a "mother in Israel," Beth Alves has much to share with the Body of Christ. She writes from a vast reservoir of wisdom and understanding gained from years of experience in the international prayer movement. Her teachings are not only practical, but very "do-able" as well. She has the wonderful ability to bring the power of prayer to where we live and walk every day. I highly recommend this book!

Jane Hansen
President/CEO, Aglow International
Edmonds, Washington

Beth Alves's *Becoming a Prayer Warrior* is one of the most practical books on prayer ever written. Full of insight and a must for every believer's library, this book will prove useful to beginning prayers and seasoned intercessors alike. I highly recommend it.

Cindy Jacobs
Cofounder, Generals of Intercession
Author, Women of Destiny *and* The Voice of God
Colorado Springs, Colorado

Beth Alves has authored a rare book. Ideal for use by individuals and prayer groups, *Becoming a Prayer Warrior* serves as both a "prayer primer" for Christians newly seeking to be effective in prayer, as well as a graduate manual for seasoned prayer warriors.

Dee Jepson
Director, Women of Faith
Port Charlotte, Florida

Beth Alves is a woman of prayer and a wonderful human being. For Beth, prayer is not theory. She lives what she writes, and she writes what she lives. In this very special book, Beth opens her heart about down-to-earth prayer that reaches heaven and assaults hell.

Gary D. Kinnaman
Senior Minister, Word of Grace
Mesa, Arizona

Practical and powerful! Wisely, Beth Alves informs, trains and equips God's army before marching us off to the spiritual wars. With strong, Spirit-led instruction, she shows you how to stand up to the devil and establish a nearly impenetrable prayer covering for yourself, your family and your leaders.

Jimmy and Carol Owens
Founders, Heal Our Land Movement
Colorado Springs, Colorado

Prayer is the key discipline whereby all spiritual work and vision is accomplished. If you are a new Christian seeking your created destiny, you must first develop a vibrant relationship with a Holy God, and *Becoming a Prayer Warrior* will help you to enter His Throne Room boldly. For you who have been prayer warriors for years, this book is like a second honeymoon!

Chuck Pierce
Director, World Prayer Center
Colorado Springs, Colorado

A sound, thoroughly scriptural, down-to-earth presentation of prayer.

John Robb
World Vision Prayer Initiatives Coordinator
Monrovia, California

A wisdom-packed manual for transforming your prayer life. *Becoming a Prayer Warrior* will cause demons to tremble as together we change the world through prayer!

Dutch Sheets
Pastor, Springs Harvest Fellowship
Colorado Springs, Colorado

Standing in the prayer gap for others is much easier when you practice what Beth Alves teaches in this excellent book. I recommend it to all who are interested in a more serious, disciplined prayer life. Thank you, Beth. You have long been a leader, teaching others how to pray more effectively. You have greatly mentored me in this area. Now you have given the Church a book to help us all grow in our communion with Him.

Quin Sherrer
Author, How to Pray for Your Children *and*
Miracles Happen When You Pray
Colorado Springs, Colorado

Beth Alves is an outstanding prayer leader and teacher. God has uniquely gifted her to teach others how to pray effectively. Join her at the feet of Jesus and you, too, will become a mighty warrior.

Mary Lance V. Sisk
Chairperson, Love Your Neighbor As Yourself USA National Committee
A.D. 2000 North American Women's Track
Charlotte, North Carolina

Christians have been called to become prayer warriors in God's army, and I know of no other person who has earned the right to be called "warrior" more than Beth Alves. I appreciate the hours and years Beth has invested in the prayer closet that, through this book, we may become the beneficiaries.

Alice Smith
Prayer Coordinator, U.S. Prayer Track of the A.D. 2000 & Beyond Movement
Houston, Texas

BECOMING A
PRAYER
WARRIOR

Elizabeth Alves

Regal

From Gospel Light
Ventura, California, U.S.A.

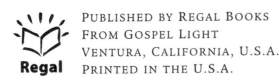

PUBLISHED BY REGAL BOOKS
FROM GOSPEL LIGHT
VENTURA, CALIFORNIA, U.S.A.
PRINTED IN THE U.S.A.

Regal Books is a ministry of Gospel Light, a Christian publisher dedicated to serving the local church. We believe God's vision for Gospel Light is to provide church leaders with biblical, user-friendly materials that will help them evangelize, disciple and minister to children, youth and families.

It is our prayer that this Regal book will help you discover biblical truth for your own life and help you meet the needs of others. May God richly bless you.

For a free catalog of resources from Regal Books/Gospel Light, please call your Christian supplier or contact us at 1-800-4-GOSPEL or www.regalbooks.com.

Cover Design by Robert Williams
Interior Design by Carolyn Henderson
Edited by Karen Kaufman

Library of Congress Cataloging-in-Publication Data
Alves, Elizabeth, 1938-
    Becoming a prayer warrior/Elizabeth Alves.
    p. cm.
    Includes bibliographical references and index.
    ISBN 0-8307-3128-8 (pbk.)
    1. Prayer—Christianity, 2. Spiritual warfare. I. Title.
BV210.2.A46 1998   98-40569
248.3 2—dc21   CIP

Formerly published by Canopy Press as *The Mighty Warrior*

18 19 20 21 22 23 24 25 26 27 28 29 / 20 19 18 17 16 15 14 13 12 11 10

Rights for publishing this book in other languages are contracted by Gospel Light Worldwide, the international nonprofit ministry of Gospel Light. Gospel Light Worldwide also provides publishing and technical assistance to international publishers dedicated to producing Sunday School and Vacation Bible School curricula and books in the languages of the world. For additional information, visit www.gospellightworldwide.org; write to Gospel Light Worldwide, P.O. Box 3875, Ventura, CA 93006; or send an e-mail to info@gospellightworldwide.org.

Dedicated to
The glory of God, the Father,
His Son and the Holy Spirit
and to
Faithful intercessors throughout the world
who stand in the gap for His leaders, continually
building a hedge of protection around them,
that kings and kingdoms might be changed
for the glory of God.

CONTENTS

Foreword

§

A great prayer movement began sweeping the world in 1970. It had been going on long before that in Korea; then God started bringing the rest of the Body of Christ on board. Pastors of all denominations in all parts of the U.S.A. are talking about prayer, teaching prayer and praying more than any other time in living memory. And the interest in prayer continues to increase. Many feel that we are now witnessing the precursor of the great revival, a worldwide outpouring of the Spirit of God on all flesh which will see vast multitudes turn to Jesus and glorify God.

I personally began to tune in to the prayer movement in 1987, making it a high agenda item for my research, writing, teaching and personal ministry. I'm rather embarrassed to admit that previous to 1987 I knew relatively little about prayer. As I began to collect a considerable amount of the available literature on prayer, one of the items I secured was *The Mighty Warrior*, at that time published in a preliminary edition. As I read it, I became very glad that Elizabeth Alves had been a long-standing participant in the prayer movement, and that she had decided to share what she had learned with those like me. This was just the book I needed. In a rare combination of thoroughness and conciseness, Beth Alves provided exactly the information I was looking for. I used it as an outline to teach some of my first lessons on prayer.

Later I found out that Beth Alves was an unusual person who

had gained a widespread reputation as one of America's foremost prayer leaders. Even before I had met her personally, I knew that she had a delightful mix of both giftedness for intercession and much experience in praying and mentoring others for prayer ministries. I have now had the privilege of knowing Beth for some time, and I greatly admire her as a person of integrity and as a woman of God.

Becoming a Prayer Warrior is the right book at the right time. The demand for a basic guidebook on all the facets of prayer is escalating rapidly because of all the Christian people who are tuning in to what the Spirit is saying to the churches about prayer these days. God is calling out a vast army of His people to pray, and they are saying, "Show me how!" I have found no better training manual than this book. It explains what prayer is, what it does, what different kinds of prayer look like, how to hear from God as you pray, the essentials of spiritual warfare and more.

Reading and applying the principles of *Becoming a Prayer Warrior* has all the potential to turn your church around and to impact your community decisively for the kingdom of God.

—C. Peter Wagner
Fuller Theological Seminary
Pasadena, California

Acknowledgments

The task of writing increases in ease and enjoyment when God provides helpers to stand beside the writer to encourage, advise and assist. I have been especially blessed in all these ways and many more. It is hard to take credit for writing a book such as this when so many people have been involved in helping to make it become a reality. Little did I know what was involved when I began to write.

It was my husband, Floyd, who provided prayer support and patiently advised, corrected and encouraged me when I thought it was an impossibility. Honey, you are the best!

Quinett Sherrer Simmons built the foundation of this book by researching the material for the original book called *The Mighty Warrior: A Guide to Effective Prayer*. When this was finished, she spent many hours helping to birth it through prayer. You are a jewel, Quinett.

Ruthanne Garlock was the initial editor. When she started, she took in a stray cat, and the next day it had seven kittens. In editing, she turned my stray into a champion and helped raise the kittens until the book took its final form and was published for the first time. You are a miracle worker, Ruthanne. Thanks for being my friend.

It was my staff who worked together in unity to see *The Mighty Warrior: A Guide to Effective Prayer* become a reality. Thank you Ron, Jo and Greg Carl, Cindy Divers, Linda Fletcher, Chris Cooper, Joanna Virden, Maury Lloyd and Barbara Myers. What tenacity!

Thank you! Thank you! Thank you!

Barbara Tommi Femrite, Russ Whitley and Carrie Hoffman teamed together to encourage and advise in the revision from my teaching manual on prayer into *The Mighty Warrior*. Such encouragers, such a gift from God.

Little did I know when it all began that someday *The Mighty Warrior* would be put into a new framework and published by a major publishing company such as Gospel Light/Renew.

To Bill Greig III and Kyle Duncan, thanks for having the confidence in me to take a self-published book and release it to the multitudes. You are awesome!

Many thanks to the Gospel Light staff for always being a blessing when I called and for opening your hearts to me in a special way. You make Gospel Light shine and make me feel so special. You know how to get to my heart!

There are not words enough in the English vocabulary to thank MY editor, Karen Kaufman, for such an outstanding job. It appears that an editor does all the work and the author gets all the credit. It just doesn't seem fair.

Thanks, Karen—you listened to my stories for hours, heard my heart and my style and put them into words in ways that would astound me. You started out my editor and ended up my friend. I will be forever grateful to you and to the Lord.

Special thanks to Pat Richardson, the Intercessors International staff (Wayne Reeves, Cindy Divers, Suzanne Tucker, June Esparza, Barbara Myers, Peggy Sweet, Maebeth Cruse, Diane Emmons, Cindy Edwards, Vicky Porterfield and Bonita Peterson) and to my prayer partners who are such a spiritual strength to me who helped birth this book into reality through many hours of prayer, and who took up the mantle to see it through this last revision. Thanks for your prayers for Karen and me and for those who have worked so hard on the publishing of this book.

So you see, this book belongs to many people and to all I am most grateful; but, nothing compares to my thanks and gratitude to the Lord Jesus Christ who allows all of us to know Him intimately through the wonderful gift of prayer.

Introduction

This book is based upon a passage from Isaiah which affirms God's work through us, His pray-ers and His intercessors, in these last days before the Lord's return:

> On your walls, O Jerusalem, I have appointed watchmen; all day and all night they will never keep silent. You who remind the Lord, take no rest for yourselves; and give Him no rest until He establishes and makes Jerusalem a praise in the earth (Isa. 62:6,7).

Jerusalem and other ancient cities had regular guards, or watchmen, who were stationed on the city walls night and day to be on the lookout for danger. They were required to call to each other every few minutes—especially in times of danger—with the cry passing from one to another entirely around the city walls. Watchmen also had a station at the gate of a city and in the adjacent tower, as well as on hilltops overlooking terraced vineyards. A watchman held a responsible office requiring much vigilance and fidelity.

The word "watchman" comes from a Hebrew root meaning "to hedge about (as with thorns); to guard, generally to protect and observe from a distance."

The modern counterpart to the Old Testament watchman is the intercessor. The city of Jerusalem is symbolic of the Church—

the Body of Christ—over which the intercessors must watch and pray until God establishes it "a praise in the earth." And just as in ancient times when an enemy would seek to destroy the leaders of a city, then take the people captive, so today we see the enemy attacking the Church by attempting to destroy its spiritual leaders.

In the Jewish tradition, a "watch" was a three-hour period; eight such watches kept guards on a constant lookout over the city for its protection. In Gethsemane, Jesus asked the disciples to keep only one-third of a watch. "He came to the disciples and found them sleeping, and said to Peter, 'So, you men could not keep watch with Me for one hour?'" (Matt. 26:40). As a result, they were totally unprepared when the betrayer and the soldiers came to arrest Jesus.

A desire to pray and communicate with the Lord and to be able to hear His voice is something that is birthed within us. Throughout the years, I have discovered that most people hear the voice of the Lord, but just don't recognize it. This can cause frustration in prayer and intercession.

Like the disciples, I found myself asking, "Lord, teach me how to pray." The Lord honored that prayer by gifting me with a mentor, the late Vinita (Nonnie) Copeland. She taught me the simplicity of prayer with dynamic results. By spending hours in prayer with her, I found prayer was not a formula but a way of life. It is as important as daily bread. It was at her feet and through her example that I found my call to intercession, and later, to the ministry that I now head, Intercessors International.

This ministry began in 1987 with the release of the first edition of the *Prayer Manual* and the recruitment of a group of intercessors who pledged to pray for missionaries, ministers and spiritual leaders. It was a small but fruitful beginning. While the leaders began to feel the impact of committed prayer coverage, the intercessors increased their vision as they saw their prayers make a difference in the lives of those on the front lines of ministry.

This book is not a set of rules and formulas. It is a guideline to help enhance your prayer life and to give you a better understanding of the basics of prayer.

I pray that reading and studying this book will help you come into a greater knowledge of Jesus, His Word and His ways, as you learn to fellowship at His feet and become a mighty warrior through prayer.

—Elizabeth Alves
Intercessors International

I Traveled on My Knees

Last night I took a journey to Israel across the seas;
    I did not go by boat or plane, I traveled on my knees.
I saw so many people there with scars and wounds
    within,
But God told me that I should go—there was oil to
    pour from Him.
I replied, "Lord, I cannot go and work with such as
    these,"
He answered quickly, "Yes you can, by traveling on
    your knees."
He said, "You pray, I'll meet their need, you call and
    I will hear,
Be concerned about the fate of those both far and
    near."
And so I tried it, knelt in prayer, gave up some
    hours of ease,
I felt the Lord right by my side while traveling on
    my knees.
As I prayed on and saw them helped, and the badly
    wounded healed,
I saw God's workers' strength renewed while
    laboring on the field.
I said, "Yes, Lord, I have a job—my desire Thy will
    to please,
I can go and heed Thy call by traveling on my
    knees."

—*Adapted from a poem by Sandra Goodwin*

Section I

The Purpose of Prayer

1

Why Pray?

Moreover, as for me, far be it from me that I should
sin against the Lord by ceasing to pray for you;
but I will instruct you in the good and right way.

—1 Samuel 12:23

It was the mid-'70s and my husband, Floyd, and I were with a group of Christian leaders called to bring the love of God to Africa. The scorching heat from the penetrating sun was nothing in comparison to the outpouring of the Son's power on the vast crowd of ebony faces and hungry hearts that stood before us. The lame began to walk; the blind received their sight. Healings of every kind were happening before our very eyes. Twenty-three thousand people were miraculously healed as God's power swept over the crowd. I remember thinking, Lord, *this is the book of Acts in action.*

As I sat on the platform watching this miraculous wave of God's power, I began to cry out to God, "Lord, why are we not seeing miracles such as these in our western culture? Is it because we are bogged down in traditions and doctrines?" I will never forget His reply:

"No, Daughter, these people are receiving because they have no fear of man."

The fear of man is our greatest detriment to knowing and serving God. Only as we lay down our worries about what people think of us and what to expect of others can God honestly and openly speak into our lives. Often we have preconceived ideas of how a person must change before he or she can come to Christ. And yet when Jesus called us to be fishers of men (and women), He told us to go out and bring them in; He did not tell us to clean up the fish before reeling them into our churches. I have never seen a fish yet who was cleaned up before it was caught.

So what is prayer and why should we pray? Do our prayers really make a difference?

The Purpose of Prayer

Christians are called to a lifestyle of prayer, but many have come to see prayer as nothing more than calling upon their Heavenly Butler for daily service, or crying out to their Heavenly Lifeguard when they are drowning in their daily circumstances. Certainly God has more for us than that. Jesus said that because He was going to the Father, we would do even greater works than He did (see John 14:12). When He spoke those words, He was not talking to a crowd of world-renowned Christian evangelists. No, He was speaking to every person who names Jesus as Lord and Savior. He was speaking to you and to me.

Prayer is the responsibility of every Christian. God's Word tells us to pray. But we don't pray just because we have to; we pray because talking to God is a privilege. Prayer is entering into relationship with God so we can determine His will in the matter and call His will into existence upon the earth. As you read the following verse, notice that talking to God on behalf of others carries a promise:

First of all, then, I urge that entreaties and prayers, petitions and thanksgivings, be made on behalf of all men, for kings and all who are in authority, *in order that we may lead a tranquil and quiet life in all godliness and dignity* (1 Tim. 2:1,2, italics added).

Much of the discontent and worry we as believers suffer is the result of disobedience to God's Word, which exhorts us to pray:

With all prayer and petition pray at all times in the Spirit, and with this in view, be on the alert with all perseverance and petition for all the saints (Eph. 6:18).

Keep watching and praying, that you may not enter into temptation; the spirit is willing, but the flesh is weak (Matt. 26:41).

Pray without ceasing (1 Thess. 5:17).

The Priority of Prayer

Prayer was the priority in Jesus' life. He considered it more important than *physical rest*, and He was commonly pictured praying all night (see Luke 6:12). Talking with the Father took priority over His social activity. Scripture often refers to Jesus going off alone to be with the Father (see Matt. 14:23; Mark 1:35; Luke 5:16; 6:12). And, finally, Jesus made prayer a priority over His *physical appetite*. He fasted for long periods of time, withdrawing from physical food to release spiritual power (see Luke 4:2; Matt. 6:18,25,31; Heb. 7:25).

Prayer was the primary communication link between Himself and the Father. Every major event and every minor decision in Jesus' life was shrouded with prayer. If we are to be Christlike, or like Christ, we must follow His example. Jesus did not pray because He had to; Jesus prayed because He wanted to be *obedient to, united with* and *empowered by* the Father. Prayer is to be our priority for those same reasons.

Someone has said that seven days without prayer makes one Christian weak. Prayer is the way that we, His branches, draw the nutrients we need from God the Vine to produce the fruit of His Spirit in our lives. And we do this because, as believers, prayer is to be our primary ministry.

The Ministry of Prayer

Ministry to God must come before ministry to people. First Peter says that you are "a chosen race, a *royal priesthood*, a holy nation, a people for God's own possession, that you may proclaim the excellencies of Him who has called you out of darkness into His marvelous light" (2:9, italics added).

The role of the priest is to minister first to God; then to the people. The way that we minister to God is by praising, worshiping and communing with Him in prayer and meditation. The way that we minister to the people is by allowing the overflow of what we have received in our time alone with Him to pour out into the lives of others. (See Prov. 15:8; 1 Pet. 2:5; Eph. 1:4,5; 2 Cor. 5:21 and Heb. 4:16.)

The Relationship of Prayer

My husband, Floyd, and I have been married for 43 years. We love each other, and because we do, it is not a chore to be together—it is an awesome privilege. We want to share and know the most intimate details of each other's lives. Although I am often the one who is out front in our ministry, Floyd is the strength behind the scenes, working to make sure that what I do when I am publicly ministering runs smoothly and effectively. This happens as we spend time communicating about our heart-felt and physical needs. We have the same goals, the same purpose, and a mutual love and respect for each other.

Similarly, the Bible says that you are Christ's Bride (see John 3:29, *NIV*). Your marital relationship with Him will deepen as you spend time alone with Him, sharing heart to heart. Prayer is that unique channel of dialogue between you and the Lord. Intimacy is cultivated as you invest time in your relationship with Him.

The result will be knowing His will and making His will known to the people. Moses is a perfect illustration of this.

There is probably no one man in the Bible who is more fully respected among the Jewish people than Moses. Why? Moses knew God; therefore, God made His ways known to Moses and His acts to the children of Israel. We read in Exodus 33:11 that "the Lord used to speak to Moses face to face, just as a man speaks to his friend." The Lord longs to speak to you today through the Holy Spirit, just as He spoke with Moses. (Read Exodus 33:11-23.) And not only does God want to speak to you, but He also wants to show you a dimension of life that is invisible to the natural eye.

The Bible says that "God is Spirit" (John 4:24). Therefore, to know and understand the things of God, your spiritual eyes need to be opened. Keenness in the Spirit realm comes as you discipline yourself in prayer, praise, fasting and renewing your mind through God's Word. Ask the Lord to reveal spiritual reality to you just as Elisha did when he asked God to open his servant's eyes, allowing him to see the chariots of protection:

So he answered, "Do not fear, for those who are with us are more than those who are with them." Then Elisha prayed and said, "O Lord, I pray, open his eyes that he may see." And the Lord opened the servant's eyes, and he saw; and behold, the mountain was full of horses and chariots of fire all around Elisha (2 Kings 6:16,17).

The more our spiritual eyes are opened, the more understanding we will have about our physical circumstances. Jesus was so spiritually attuned that He said:

"Who is the one who touched Me?" And while they were all denying it, Peter said, "Master, the multitudes are crowding and pressing upon You." But Jesus said, "Someone did touch Me, for I was aware that power had gone out of Me" (Luke 8:45,46).

Peter was looking at the natural touch; Jesus was aware that something was happening in the spiritual realm. Prayer ignites our natural senses so the light of His Spirit is able to shine in on the motives of the power and principalities at work around us.

The Sacrifice of Prayer

The Scripture tells us that Jesus went to the cross for the joy set before Him. How can this be? How could the Cross possibly have brought Him joy? Because when Jesus was on earth, He was limited by time and distance. Through His death and Resurrection, however, He was able to send the Comforter so all believers could have ongoing, immediate access to the Father via the Holy Spirit. Romans 8:34 says that "Christ Jesus is He who died, yes, rather who was raised, who is at the right hand of God, who also intercedes for us."

Prayer is a love response to the burdens of others.

As we follow Christ's example, we too must freely give ourselves to prayer. Prayer is an unselfish work that is often unseen and unappreciated by others; they only experience the results. When we pray, we are not seeking to be seen by men, but rather to stand in the presence and pleasure of the Lord (see Matt. 6:5; Heb. 7:25). Our times with God the Father bring us into oneness of heart with Him. We are then able to experience His heartache over the lost, His compassion for the hurting and His love for others—even our enemies.

Prayer is a love response to the burdens of others. The apostle Paul set forth a model for unselfish prayer in Philippians 2:3,4:

Do nothing from selfishness or empty conceit, but with humility of mind let each of you regard one another as more important than himself; do not merely look out for your own personal interests, but also for the interests of others.

The apostle said he did not cease giving thanks for others while making mention of them in his prayers (see Eph. 1:15,16; Phil. 1:3,4,7). Paul, like Jesus, believed God. As a result, prison gates were opened, souls were saved, the afflicted were healed and lives were transformed. Prayer is powerful, especially when it is based upon God's Word.

The Word of Prayer

As you spend time talking with the Father and reading His Word, your prayers will begin to reflect the heart, mind and Word of the Lord. God's Word is the same yesterday, today and forever. God will meet you right where you are, using the amount of knowledge you have. For example, I remember when a woman who had just become a Christian once called for prayer, saying that her baby had a stubborn diaper rash that would not respond to medication. I told her to "apply the Word of God" and call me with the answer. Twenty-four hours later, she called to say that her baby was cured. When I asked her which verse she had prayed, she explained that she had ripped a page out of the Word and placed it in her baby's diaper each time she changed it. God met this young mom right where she was, with the knowledge that she had!

Ask God to give you a verse that applies to the situation for which you are praying, and pray it. For example, you might pray Colossians 1 by inserting your own name or the name of your family and friends, asking "that you may be filled with the knowledge of His will in all spiritual wisdom and understanding, so that you may walk in a manner worthy of the Lord, to please Him in all respects, bearing fruit in every good work and increasing in the knowledge of God; strengthened with all power, according to His glorious might, for the attaining of all steadfastness and patience; joyously giving thanks to the Father, who has qualified us to share in the inheritance of the saints in light" (vv. 9-12).

Your prayer will then become God's own Word alive in your mouth. Praying God's Word brings results and answers, because

God Himself said that His Word will not return to Him empty, without accomplishing what He desires, and without succeeding in the matter for which He sent it (see Isa. 55:11). When you pray the Word, however, it must be quickened by the Holy Spirit so you may speak forth with anointing.

Do not pray the Word for the sake of religious activity. Pray the Word based on faith, believing that you are in agreement with God's will for the circumstance. Let faith be the motivation behind your prayer. Then you will have the assurance that He will work in cooperation with you:

> And without faith it is impossible to please Him, for he who comes to God must believe that He is, and that He is a rewarder of those who seek Him (Heb. 11:6).

Prayer that is based on faith bears fruit for the Kingdom and pleases God. When you pray and communicate with God in faith, He will speak to you and give you direction, wisdom, knowledge, strength and protection (see Col. 1:9-11; Ps. 40:1,2; John 15:7,8).

The Kingdom Partnership of Prayer

Prayer makes a way for God to act sovereignly on earth. Jesus said to pray, "Thy will be done, on earth as it is in heaven" (Matt. 6:10). God has chosen to work through people, not around them. Therefore, He also says, "Truly I say to you, whatever you shall bind on earth shall be bound in heaven; and whatever you loose on earth shall be loosed in heaven" (Matt. 18:18). The obvious inference is that God has limited some of His activities on the earth and will respond only to the prayers of His children.

Heaven waits for those of us on earth to pray for things to happen. E. Stanley Jones once said, "We align ourselves with the purpose and power of God, and He is able to do things through us that He could not do otherwise." God seeks for a person, an intercessor, to plead for His perfect will to be done on earth as it is in heaven (see Isa. 43.26; Jer. 1:12).

Prayer Versus Intercession

At this point you may be asking, *What is the difference between prayer and intercession?* Prayer starts *with you* and what you know to be the obvious facts as you bring them before God. God will then take over and you will pray what is on your heart and mind until you have prayed it through. Many times prayer will lead to intercession, where God takes over and you are praying in ways you do not understand for that person.

Intercession differs from prayer in that it starts and ends *with God.* You might be driving along and someone will come to your mind, maybe a sense of urgency about a friend or relative, or even a person you haven't thought about in years. This is God speaking to you. Sometimes you won't understand why you are praying what you are praying, but as you are obedient to pray what you are sensing, God's will is done on earth. Sometimes God will allow you to know the outcome; other times He won't. Your responsibility is to be obedient.

An example of this from my own life involves a favorite cousin I hadn't seen in about 10 years. I crawled out of bed in the middle of the night for a glass of water when a picture of my cousin canvassed my mind. Suddenly I dropped to my knees and began to cry out, "God, don't let Mike move! Keep him still, Lord! Keep him still! Oh God, please don't let him move! Hold him, Lord! Hold him!"

Even though I was pleading on Mike's behalf with my words, I remember thinking, *This is really ridiculous. Why am I praying this?* Then the words ceased, and when they did, I could not muster another word. So I got up, drank a glass of water and started back toward the bedroom. Again I fell to the floor and began to cry out with a grave sense of urgency, "Don't let him move, God! Don't let Mike move! Stay still! Stay still!" The words came to an abrupt end. This time I thought, *Oh no! This must be a nightmare!*

I had no feeling inside of me other than the feeling to pray. I got up and began to pace the floor, wondering what in the world that was all about. One more time I took a few steps toward the bedroom when again I dropped to the floor. Only this time I was yelling, "Get him up, Lord! Get him to run! Run, Mike! Lord, help him to run... run...run! Let him run, God! Run, run, run!" After several minutes, a calm came over me and I returned to bed for the night.

The following day, I called my aunt to see if she could help me put the pieces together about my puzzling outcries the night before. She informed me that Mike was in Vietnam. The experience still made very little sense.

Finally, a month later my aunt called to read a letter she had received. The letter told how Mike, who was a pilot, had been shot down and landed in a tree. He had been warned to get out of the area as quickly as possible, but explained that just a few hundred yards from the crash site, he fell into a bush. "Mom," he wrote, "it was like I was pinned down. I felt like somebody was sitting on me. The Vietcong came and were unknowingly standing on my pant leg while looking up at my parachute in the tree. They turned around and began to slash the bushes with their bayonets. It looked safe, so I started to get up and was about to run when once again I fell into the bush as though someone were pushing me. I laid there for a couple of minutes when suddenly I had an impulse to get up and run. I heard a helicopter so I sprinted through the wooded area, following the direction of the noise, to an open space where I was whisked off to safety. The helicopter crew said they came in response to my beeper. And yet, it had not been working when I was shot down." That, dear ones, is intercession!

The Power of Prayer

Prayer can cause God to relent. Many times the fate of the world is not in the hands of governors or kings, but in the hands of mighty intercessors. You, too, can influence society as did Abraham and Daniel and others in the Old Testament (see Gen.

18:17-30; Num. 14:11-23; 1 Sam. 7:8-13; 2 Kings 20:1-11; Dan. 9:2,3). It is exciting to realize that your prayers not only affect those you are praying for, but can also help to mold national or international events. As you read the following passage, notice how God changed His mind based on Moses' prayer:

> Then Moses entreated the Lord his God, and said, "O Lord, why doth Thine anger burn against Thy people whom Thou hast brought out from the land of Egypt with great power and with a mighty hand? Why should the Egyptians speak, saying, 'With evil intent He brought them out to kill them in the mountains and to destroy them from the face of the earth'? Turn from Thy burning anger and change Thy mind about doing harm to Thy people. Remember Abraham, Isaac, and Israel, Thy servants to whom Thou didst swear by Thyself, and didst say to them, 'I will multiply your descendants as the stars of the heavens, and all this land of which I have spoken I will give to your descendants, and they shall inherit it forever.'" So the Lord changed His mind about the harm which He said He would do to His people (Exod. 32:11-14).

Not only does the Lord change His mind when His people pray, but He also gives revelation knowledge and the mind of God through His Holy Spirit. As you pray, He will pinpoint a problem area in someone's life or in a situation, allowing you to see as He sees. Luke tells us that "all things have been handed over to Me by My Father, and no one knows who the Son is except the Father, and who the Father is except the Son, and anyone *to whom the Son wills to reveal Him*" (10:22, italics added). The role of intercession is a sacred trust. The intercessor must carefully guard the secrets God reveals during prayer and be obedient to share only when the Lord directs. Seek His clear guidance on the proper follow-up of His revelation (see Matt. 11:25,26; Phil. 3:15).

As you continue in prayer, the kingdom of God will become real through the miracles of God operating in your life. You will see the manifest power of God confirm your spiritual walk. Jesus said that "these signs will accompany those who have believed: in My name they will cast out demons, they will speak with new tongues; they will pick up serpents, and if they drink any deadly poison, it shall not hurt them; they will lay hands on the sick, and they will recover" (Mark 16:17,18). Do not be afraid to believe God for the miraculous.

The Warfare of Prayer

But remember, you have an enemy. Ephesians tells us that "our struggle is not against flesh and blood, but against the rulers, against the powers, against the world forces of this darkness, against the spiritual forces of wickedness in the heavenly places" (6:12).

You are called to do spiritual warfare through prayer over Satan's strongholds until you win! Satan will usually attack us most in our greatest area of strength. I used to think the reverse was true—that he would attack most in our area of greatest weakness. But I have found that in our areas of weakness, we are more apt to call upon the Lord and rely upon Him. In our areas of strength, however, we tend to rely on self and often find ourselves burning out from fighting our battles alone. Every area of your life is subject to enemy attack, so you must fight on your knees before you can stand on your mission field.

Jesus Himself had to battle Satan through prayer for His ministry and in other situations. We find this clearly illustrated in His wilderness temptation. He experienced spiritual warfare and won before He ever went out into public ministry. You, too, must win before you can fully function in what God has called you to do. The success of your Christian life is dependent on winning... winning in prayer (see Josh. 1:3,11,15; Matt. 4:11; Mark 3:27).

Daniel's spiritual battle clearly illustrates the war that occurs in the heavenlies:

Then he said to me, "Do not be afraid, Daniel, for from the first day that you set your heart on understanding this and on humbling yourself before your God, your words were heard, and I have come in response to your words. But the prince of the kingdom of Persia was withstanding me for twenty-one days; then behold, Michael, one of the chief princes, came to help me, for I had been left there with the kings of Persia" (Dan. 10:12,13).

Daniel's story gives hope for those who are in the midst of battle. Don't give up. You are in a win-win situation. God is for you, and the battle is the Lord's.

The Invitation of Prayer

Prayer is not just a call to war; it is also an invitation to rest. Jesus said, "Be anxious for nothing, but in everything by prayer and supplication with thanksgiving let your requests be made known to God. And the peace of God, which surpasses all comprehension, shall guard your hearts and your minds in Christ Jesus" (Phil. 4:6,7).

Knowing that God is on your side will help you to enter into the rest He offers. He invites you to give Him your problems, cares, concerns and worries (see 1 Pet. 5:7; Matt. 6:25,26). "Cast your burden upon [Him], and He will sustain you; He will never allow the righteous to be shaken" (Ps. 55:22). Cease striving and partner with Him. He loves you and longs to share His heart with you. He has called you, dear child of God, to rest in His love as you come away with Him in prayer. Will you say yes to that invitation today?

2

Teach Me to Pray

And He said to him, "You shall love the Lord
your God with all your heart, and with all your
soul, and with all your mind."

—*Matthew 22:37*

In 1970 I went through an experience that brought me into a rekindled sense of God's presence. The Lord in His ultimate wisdom raised up a godly mentor for me who was dedicated to prayer. She talked to God the Father, God the Son and God the Holy Spirit as if they were right there with her. I so longed for that kind of intimacy with the Lord that I spent the next three years sitting at her feet and following her example.

Because I had come from a liturgical background, I felt awkward with much of the body language I saw my mentor use as she poured out her heart to God in prayer. Lifting my hands was especially difficult in the beginning because our church did not do that. As I read through the Scriptures, however, I found verse after verse about lifting my hands to the Lord (see Pss. 28:2; 63:4; 119:48; 134:2; 143:6). I realized my struggle was not as much with God as it was with tradition and my fear of man: *What would people think of me?*

My self-consciousness ended one Sunday morning in church when I lowered my hands because I thought someone was watching me. Suddenly a little five-year-old boy loudly exclaimed, "Mommy, why does that lady raise her hands down to praise the devil instead of up to praise Jesus?" That did it! I threw my hands into the air. From that day forward, I began to pray with uplifted hands and a new sense of purpose in my heart.

As I watched my spiritual mother walk, lie, kneel and move about with an intense spirit of worship, I, too, began to minister to the King of kings and Lord of lords with my whole heart and body. People often ask me, "How long, where and in what position should I pray?" As we look at some of these basic questions, remember that the issue is not as much time, place or position as it is faithfulness to God.

How Long Do I Pray?

My mentor's son was an evangelist for whom I served, doing household chores. Throughout the day I would stop to pray with him and his wife, and we saw many miraculous answers. Eventually the evangelist decided to rent a house to use for prayer. He asked me if I would be willing to pray between four and six hours a day. Excitedly, I responded, "I'll take six!"

The evangelist wisely suggested I start with four, and I'm glad he did. I'll never forget that first day. I walked into the prayer house, closed the door behind me and sighed, "Oh Lord, here we are, just You and me." I dropped to the floor and began to pour my heart out in prayer. I prayed and prayed until I found myself laying there in a state of exhaustion. When I looked at my watch, I thought the battery was running down. Could it be that I had only prayed for 15 minutes! I began again. I prayed for everyone I knew. Then I prayed the Lord's prayer—I even sang the Lord's prayer. I looked at my watch again, only 42 minutes had passed. I couldn't believe it! Finally I cried out to God, "Lord, teach me to pray."

I understood for the first time the frustration and anxieties of

Jesus' disciples, who walked with Him daily but knew that they did not have what He had in terms of communication with the Father. Each one of us must come to a point where we too cry out to God, "Lord, teach me to pray." Learning to pray begins by making the choice to be alone with Him.

The account of Jesus and His disciples at Gethsemane clearly shows that Jesus did not hesitate to ask His followers to pray with Him for "one hour," and that this was a perfectly legitimate request. Yet, at the time He most needed and desired their support, they disappointed Him. Surely it must still disappoint our Lord when His followers put sleep and other activities above a desire to pray and spend time with Him.

One pastor has said, "When you come to the place where you can tarry with the Lord one hour, something supernatural happens. You begin to understand the character and purposes of God, and to experience the anointing of the power of God as never before."

If making a commitment to pray one hour a day seems too difficult, begin by praying 15 minutes a day, then strive to increase your prayer time.

As you pray, a basic question may come to mind: *How long should I spend for each person or subject?* The following are some suggestions:

- Pray until an answer is received and you literally see the fulfillment of it come to pass.

or

- Pray until you have the assurance from the Lord that what you have asked has been accomplished in the spiritual realm. How? By exhausting your efforts or until you have peace. Then accept the answer by faith. When you do your part in intercession, you must trust God's timing. He is never late—though it seems to His children that He passes up many opportunities to be early!
- Once you have prayed through your daily strategy, praise is always in order. Give Him praise and thanksgiving for the victory gained.

If an answer is long in coming, be tenacious and follow the example of the widow in Luke 18:

> Now He was telling them a parable to show that at all times they ought to pray and not to lose heart, saying, "There was in a certain city a judge who did not fear God, and did not respect man. And there was a widow in that city, and she kept coming to him, saying, 'Give me legal protection from my opponent.' And for a while he was unwilling; but afterward he said to himself, 'Even though I do not fear God nor respect man, yet because this widow bothers me, I will give her legal protection, lest by continually coming she wear me out.'" And the Lord said, "Hear what the unrighteous judge said; now shall not God bring about justice for His elect, who cry to Him day and night, and will He delay long over them? I tell you that He will bring about justice for them speedily. However, when the Son of Man comes, will He find faith on the earth?" (vv. 1-8).

Prayer is only vain repetition when you speak empty words without faith behind them, or if you ask with a wrong motivation.

The word "bothers" (see v. 5) comes from a Greek word meaning "to beat the breast in grief; to lament or mourn; to give trouble to." The idea is to pray persistently and tenaciously.

When a response is delayed, continue to hold fast in prayer, like the widow in Luke 18. Do not cast away your confidence as you wait on the Lord; if you grow weary and give up, the fruit of your prayer can be aborted (see Gal. 6:9). Remember the words of Jesus:

> "Ask, and it shall be given to you; seek, and you shall find; knock, and it shall be opened to you. For everyone who

asks, receives; and he who seeks finds and to him who knocks it shall be opened (Matt. 7:7,8).

Therefore, keep on asking, keep on seeking, keep on knocking—keep on!

Is all this asking what the Bible refers to as "vain repetitions" or lack of faith? No! This kind of repetition is not wrong as long as it is spoken in faith. Prayer is only vain repetition when you speak empty words without faith behind them, or if you ask with a wrong motivation (see Jas. 4:3).

Jesus Himself gives us a good example of being tenacious and asking with the right motive. During His Gethsemane ordeal, it is written that Jesus specifically prayed, "My Father, if it is possible, let this cup pass from Me; yet not as I will, but as Thou wilt" (Matt. 26:39).

Jesus made this same request three times:

And again He went away and prayed, saying the same words (Mark 14:39).

And He left them again, and went away and prayed a third time, saying the same thing once more (Matt. 26:44).

Charles Spurgeon said, "By perseverance the snail reached the ark."[1] Keep praying until the Lord says it's time to quit!

When Do I Pray?

My husband, Floyd, springs out of bed every morning eager to spend time in prayer with God. By spending those early hours with Jesus, Floyd is giving the very best of his day to the Lord. I, on the other hand, pray best between the hours of midnight and 3 A.M. God has called me to be on the midnight watch. I jokingly tell Floyd the airwaves are less crowded on my watch! Your prayer watch may be in the middle of the day. God deals with each of us individually.

When the Holy Spirit calls you to pray, let nothing stand in your way. Be like the psalmist who wrote, "As for me, I shall call upon God, and the Lord will save me. *Evening* and *morning* and at *noon*, I will complain and murmur, and He will hear my voice" (Ps. 55:16,17, italics added). Obey the urgency of the Spirit to pray immediately when you feel an inner witness. An immediate response can change the direction of a person's life, or a situation, for the purpose of God's glory and another's good.

You can accomplish far more through prayer than through your works and deeds. You are meeting with God Himself, asking for divine intervention. Procrastination can be your greatest enemy, so use your time wisely—don't waste it.

The "when" of your prayer time is between you and God. He knows your schedule and when you will be most effective. What matters most is that you set aside time each day to meet with Him.

As you study the following Scriptures and biblical examples, ask God for the specific time He wants you to intercede.

Morning

Psalm 5:3	Psalm 88:13	Mark 1:35

Acts 2:1-4,15 (Note: the Holy Spirit fell at 9 A.M.)

Noon

Psalm 55:17

Evening

Matthew 14:23	Luke 6:12	Mark 6:47
Acts 16:25		

Continuously

1 Samuel 7:8	Romans 1:9,10	1 Samuel 12:23
Ephesians 6:18	Nehemiah 1:6	Colossians 1:9
Psalm 72:15	Colossians 4:2	Luke 2:37
1 Thessalonians 3:10	Luke 6:12	1 Thessalonians 5:17
Acts 10:2	Timothy 5:5	

Keep in mind that Jesus prayed early in the mornings and often all night! There is never a wrong time to pray (see 1 Thess. 5:17); but it's important to keep our appointments with God.

Where Do I Pray?

Just as some work environments are more productive than others, the place where we pray can make a difference. Ask the Lord to show you where He wants to meet with you. If you have a specific place where you go to meet with Him, your prayer time will be more effective. Some people have a special chair or a particular room where they pray daily. Many men have told me they like to pray outside. A friend who is a pastor in Holland took me to a tree where he spends his prayer time every morning. The tree is so enormous that it would take three people to wrap their arms around it, so the tree provides protection from the elements. My friend said that no matter what the weather is like, he meets God at the tree every morning.

When I first began to hear the Holy Spirit speak to me, I was in the bathtub. It was such a powerful experience that I thought I had to be in the tub to hear Him. I remember feeling anxious and agitated if I couldn't take a bath everytime I had a problem or a question. I guess you could say God was "cleaning up my act"!

Today I meet with God in a little prayer house on the property of our ministry, Intercessors International. It is a place where I am not easily distracted. There I have a chair that I feel is my holy place with God.

The Bible gives many examples of places to pray. And the place becomes sacred when you remove yourself from the world and enter into His presence:

> And when you pray, you are not to be as the hypocrites; for they love to stand and pray in the synagogues and on the street corners, in order to be seen by men. Truly I say to you, they have their reward in full. But you, when you pray, go into your inner room, and when you have shut

your door, pray to your Father who is in secret, and your
Father who sees in secret will repay you (Matt. 6:5,6).

"Secret" means "concealed from public view or from general
knowledge; operating in a hidden or confidential manner."

The "inner room," or inner chamber, was usually an upper
story built on the roof of a house. It was strategically located on
the city walls facing or overlooking the city gate. The chamber
could be used as a watchtower to spot the enemy or observe a
victory parade. It was also a high place for an altar and a place of
prayer.

When you participate in inner chamber prayer, the Word
states that the Father will reward you openly. However, you do
not have to be in an inner room to be in communion with the
Lord. You can be in a park, on a train, driving on the highway or
just about anywhere with others all around you when the Holy
Spirit nudges you to pray. While driving in traffic, you can practice "intersection intercession."

The Bible mentions many places people prayed, but the following are a few referred to in the New Testament:

Upper room . . . . .Acts 1:13,14

House . . . . .Acts 10:30; 12:5-17

By a river . . . . .Acts 16:13

On a beach . . . . .Acts 21:5

Wilderness . . . . .Luke 5:16

Lonely place . . . . .Mark 1:35; Luke 4:42

Mountains . . . . .Matthew 14:23; Mark 6:46;
                             Luke 5:16; 6:12; 9:28; John 6:15

Alone . . . . .Matthew 6:6; 26:39; Mark 6:46;
                             14:32-42; Luke 6:12; 9:18; 22:41

Even though it's important to set aside a scheduled time and
place to be alone for prayer, be on prayer alert at all times
because the Holy Spirit may quicken you to a special concern
that needs immediate prayer, regardless of where you are.

In What Position Do I Pray?

Just as there are various places to pray, there are also a variety of postures for prayer. As I began to travel the nations, I discovered that within many denominations, tradition often dictates the way people position their bodies for prayer. For example, when I first moved to Germany, I noticed that people would not sit while praying. They believed sitting was disrepectful to God. I have since come to realize that many nations are influenced by church traditions that have similar standards, such as kneeling or standing.

Because I grew up with a liturgical background, I too used to believe that I could only pray if I knelt. Although I still enjoy kneeling at times, I have since discovered that worship can encompass many physical positions. Our physical position should be a response to the leading of the Holy Spirit. Usually when we are caught up in ministering to the Lord, we will just naturally respond outwardly to the inward position of our hearts before God.

The following are some examples of positions listed in the Bible. By practicing the style that you feel least comfortable with, you can experience a breakthrough that can change your life.

Here are some examples listed in the Bible:

SITTING
1 Chronicles 17:16-27

KNEELING
1 Kings 8:54; Ezra 9:5;
Luke 22:41; Acts 9:40

BOWING
Exodus 34:8; Nehemiah 8:6; Psalm 72:11

Here are some examples listed in the Bible (continued):

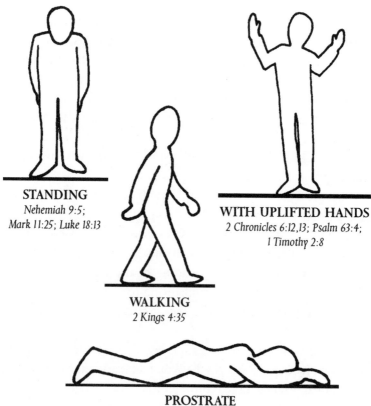

STANDING
Nehemiah 9:5;
Mark 11:25; Luke 18:13

WALKING
2 Kings 4:35

WITH UPLIFTED HANDS
2 Chronicles 6:12,13; Psalm 63:4;
1 Timothy 2:8

PROSTRATE
Joshua 7:6; Ezra 10:1; Matthew 26:39; Mark:14:35

Whether you sit, stand, bow or kneel, it is the position of your heart that matters most. Whatever you do, do it as unto the Lord and always be careful not to make a ritual out of your worship to God.

If Jesus were you today, how would He live His life through you? The right response to that question will make all that you do His answered prayer.

Note

1. John L. Mason, *An Enemy Called Average* (Tulsa, Okla.: Harrison House, 1990), p. 20.

3

Types of Prayer

And this is the confidence which we have
before Him, that, if we ask anything
according to His will, He hears us.

—1 John 5:14

Effective prayer begins with recognizing that you are entering into the very presence of God for the purpose of building relationship with Him. And relationships that work are built with praise, gratitude, honesty, trust, forgiveness and intimacy. In other words, they are motivated by love. Therefore, the way that you pray should reflect these same relational elements.

As you read through the following pages and study the various types of prayer, remember that your time with God is about relationship. Resist the temptation to become ritualistic and focus instead on your love for Him.

Praise and Thanksgiving

Praise and thanksgiving open our hearts and cause joy to well up in our spirits. The Word tells us that praise and thanksgiving are Kingdom keys that open the doors to His courts, allowing us to enter into His presence:

Enter His gates with thanksgiving, and His courts with
praise. Give thanks to Him; bless His name (Ps. 100:4).

As you enter into praise, meditate on the provision the Lord
has made for you through the blood of Jesus. His blood allows
you to walk today in the new covenant (see Heb. 10:19; 12:24).

Praise God for Who He Is!
The source of praise is the Holy Spirit activating your spirit to
express approval and adoration for God's greatness. As you read
through the Scriptures, keep a list of the qualities that you discover about Him: His mercy, His faithfulness, His patience, His
everlasting love. Praise Him for His character. Develop the habit
of praise during your prayer time.

O Lord, open my lips, that my mouth may declare Thy
praise (Ps. 51:15).

Seven times a day I praise Thee, because of Thy righteous
ordinances (Ps. 119:164).

As you begin to praise and extol the Lord, your spirit rises up
within you to increase your understanding of who He is. Your
soul is also strengthened in the process of praise because praise
causes faith to grow, and as it grows, you suddenly realize that
nothing is too difficult for Him (see Jer. 32:17).

Thank Him for What He Has Done and Will Continue to Do
Thanksgiving awakens your love toward God as you acknowledge
that you are His child. Thank Him that He gives you every good
and perfect gift (see Jas. 1:17). Respond with joy to His benefits
showered on you as His heir.

In all your ways acknowledge Him, and He will make your
paths straight (Prov. 3:6).

What shall I render to the Lord for all His benefits toward

me? To Thee I shall offer a sacrifice of thanksgiving, and call upon the name of the Lord (Ps. 116:12,17).

An attitude of gratitude washes away negativity and purifies your soul.

Praise Application:
With these thoughts, begin to *praise* and *thank* Him. Express your love and adoration for Him. Acknowledge His attributes through His different names. (See "The Names of God," chapter 9.)

The following are seven Hebrew expressions of praise from the Old Testament:

- **Towdah:** Sacrifice of thanksgiving or praise; to render thanksgiving or praise. (See Pss. 42:4; 100:4.)
- **Yadah:** To throw, thrust or cast away from, hands outward, to throw hands into the air. (See Pss. 67:3; 107:8, 15,21,31.)
- **Barak:** To bless, to give thanks and praise to God because He has given out of His abundance; bless as an act of adoration, to kneel. (See Pss. 31:21; 63:4; 95:6.)
- **Halal:** To make a show or boast, to be clamorously foolish, to go about in a raging or raving way, to dance, to celebrate. (See Pss. 56:4; 150:1,2.)
- **Zamar:** To celebrate with instruments, to praise the Lord skillfully on an instrument, to touch strings with the fingers. (See Pss. 21:13; 33:2; 98:4.)
- **Tehillah:** An imperative summons to praise Jehovah. A psalm or a hymn, by choirs, with dancing and expressive speaking; festal jubilation. (See Pss. 22:3,25; 33:1; 35:28.)
- **Shabach:** Praise, comment; adoration toward the power, glory and sanctity of the Lord. Praise God for His mighty acts and deeds. To triumph in a loud voice. (See Pss. 63:3,4; 117:1; 147:12.)

A joyful way to start a prayer time is to choose a psalm or several verses from the Bible and read each expression of praise out loud. This will energize your spirit. Psalms 145—150 are especially good because they exalt God for His goodness, love, power, holiness, wisdom, greatness, glory and majesty.

Start with Psalm 145:1-7:

> I will extol Thee, my God, O King; and I will bless Thy
> name forever and ever. Every day I will bless Thee, and I
> will praise Thy name forever and ever. Great is the Lord,
> and highly to be praised; and His greatness is unsearch-
> able. One generation shall praise Thy works to another,
> and shall declare Thy mighty acts. On the glorious splen-
> dor of Thy majesty, and on Thy wonderful works, I will
> meditate. And men shall speak of the power of Thine awe-
> some acts; and I will tell of Thy greatness...and shall shout
> joyfully of Thy righteousness.

Thanksgiving Application:

The following is an adaptation of Psalm 136. It is an effective tool
for motivating you in thanksgiving toward the Lord.

> I give thanks to You, Lord, for (name a person). Your
> lovingkindness is everlasting. I give thanks to You, Lord,
> who has given (list a material blessing). Your lovingkind-
> ness is everlasting. I give thanks to You, Lord, who has
> given (list a spiritual blessing). Your lovingkindness is ever-
> lasting. I give thanks to You, Lord, who has heard my prayer
> for (list something you are asking for). Your lovingkindness
> is everlasting. I give thanks to You, Lord, who has answered
> my prayer for (you fill in). Your lovingkindness is everlast-
> ing. I give thanks to You, Lord, who has (you fill in). Your lov-
> ingkindness is everlasting. I give thanks to You, Lord, who
> has (you fill in). Your lovingkindness is everlasting. I give
> thanks to You, Lord, who has (you fill in). Your lov-
> ingkindness is everlasting. I give thanks to You, Lord, who
> has (you fill in). Your lovingkindness is everlasting.

Confession and Forgiveness

Confession and forgiveness are the appropriate responses to the
holiness of God. You must set your will to have a pure, undivid-

ed heart and a right attitude toward every person, including the Lord God. This is a prerequisite to effective intercession!

You can confess your sins for hours on end, but confession is not complete unless it is coupled with forgiveness. "Confession" means "to acknowledge or disclose something damaging or inconvenient to one's self; to acknowledge or admit something." "Forgiveness" means "to excuse a fault or offense; to pardon; to relinquish anger, resentment or bitterness against a person; to absolve from payment of."

So you see, one is not complete without the other. After confession and forgiveness, you must go one step further and receive the provisions God has granted you through His Word, such as healing, peace and prosperity. Many people confess and forgive, but they make the mistake of not receiving God's special promises because they feel unworthy. This is a false concept. God's promises are a special gift to you.

Learn to be a good receiver. Receiving means to acquire or take something offered or given. Receiving requires action on your part. Quote God's promises aloud and accept them by faith, not relying on your feelings or emotions.

Through this process of confession and forgiveness you are restored to fellowship. Praise the Lord for His blood which ransoms you and pays your debt.

Now let's discuss both confession and forgiveness separately:

Confession
Read the following Scripture carefully:

> Behold, the Lord's hand is not so short that it cannot save; neither is His ear so dull that it cannot hear. But your iniquities have made a separation between you and your God, and your sins have hidden His face from you, so that He does not hear (Isa. 59:1,2).

Did you notice that iniquities can cause your prayers to go unheard? Confession must take place before you enter into intercession or petition so that your prayers are pleasing to God's ears.

You cannot be purified in your own power and strength. But God provides the Holy Spirit to shine on your sins so you can confess them. During your prayer time, pause and ask the Holy Spirit if there is any matter that needs to be confessed. Then respond to Him with your answer.

> Examine me, O Lord, and try me; test my mind and my heart. For Thy lovingkindness is before my eyes, and I have walked in Thy truth (Ps. 26:2,3).

Once an area of darkness has been brought to the light of God's Word and repented of, don't look back. When a sin has been dealt with, know that the power of Jesus' blood covers it and the Lord refuses to remember it. Don't try to bring up past sins that have already been covered by the blood. The Lord has buried them in the depths of the sea and they are forgotten. Meditate instead on the following Scriptures:

> If we confess our sins, He is faithful and righteous to forgive us our sins and to cleanse us from all unrighteousness (1 John 1:9).

> It was for freedom that Christ set us free; therefore keep standing firm and do not be subject again to a yoke of slavery (Gal. 5:1).

> If we say that we fellowship with Him and yet walk in the darkness, we lie and do not practice the truth; but if we walk in the light as He Himself is in the light, we have fellowship with one another, and the blood of Jesus His Son cleanses us from all sin (1 John 1:6,7).

> He will again have compassion on us; He will tread our iniquities under foot. Yes, Thou wilt cast all their sins into the depths of the sea (Mic. 7:19).

Be aware of Satan's tactics to bring you into condemnation or guilt by reminding you of past sins. Through introspection, he desires that you keep your mind centered on yourself and away from praying, praising and pulling down his strongholds. The battleground is your mind:

> For the weapons of our warfare are not of the flesh, but divinely powerful for the destruction of fortresses. We are destroying speculations and every lofty thing raised up against the knowledge of God, and we are taking every thought captive to the obedience of Christ, and we are ready to punish all disobedience, whenever your obedience is complete (2 Cor. 10:4-6).

We must choose to let God's peace guard our hearts and minds daily through Jesus Christ to prevent this struggle. If our hearts condemn us, then we cannot ask in faith. We are double minded and cannot pray in confidence (see Jas. 1:6). Peace of mind comes by continual prayer:

> Be anxious for nothing, but in everything by prayer and supplication with thanksgiving let your requests be made known to God. And the peace of God, which surpasses all comprehension, shall guard your hearts and your minds in Christ Jesus (Phil. 4:6,7).

When confessing your sins, know that you need not have an emotional experience to be forgiven. First ask; then accept by faith in God's Word that He will do exactly as He says...that He is "faithful and just" to forgive you (1 John 1:9, *KJV*).

Forgiveness

Unforgiveness breaks your full communication with the Lord. It desensitizes you to spiritual things.

When you ask forgiveness for yourself and those who have sinned against you, you will be set free and able to walk in right relationship with God and man. Forgiveness also frees the other person, or changes the circumstances that are causing the problem. It allows the Holy Spirit to do His job, which is to bring conviction about the sin so righteousness can be restored.

If you are having a problem forgiving someone, determine to obey God's Word and refuse to be guided by your feelings. Do not let pride keep you from having a right relationship with God. Lay down your hurts, self-righteous attitude and hostilities. Forgive the person who has wronged you, no matter how unjust the offense may be. You will then experience a release in your spirit, and your feelings will begin to follow. Your fellowship with the Lord will then be restored.

There are three areas of unforgiveness:

1. *Unforgivenss toward people* who have hurt or offended you.
2. *Unforgiveness toward God* because in your perception He did not intervene on your behalf in the way you wanted Him to.
3. *Unforgivenss toward yourself* for situations you have experienced or participated in that cause you hurt, guilt, condemnation, worry, frustration, pity or shame.

God's Word says, "For if you forgive men for their transgressions, your heavenly Father will also forgive you. But if you do not forgive men, then your Father will not forgive your transgressions" (Matt. 6:14,15). I have discovered that most people find it fairly easy to forgive others, very difficult to forgive God, and almost impossible to forgive themselves. Total forgiveness, however, is essential to your effective praying.

Make a decision every morning that you will walk in forgiveness throughout the day. Do not wait until you get into a confrontation and then try to forgive the person who has wronged you. Choose to forgive others as God has forgiven you, and do it at the time of the offense, just as Jesus did (see Luke 23:34).

Forgiveness in itself is not enough; you must also repent. To repent is to feel such regret or remorse that you turn away from your thoughts or actions and release others from any bondage you or they hold. Unless this is done, you will never be free. Forgiveness and repentance go hand in hand (see Prov. 28:13; Matt. 3:6,8). When we say that we have forgiven, but we are still holding on to wrong attitudes, we rebel against God.

When our daughter Peggy was about four years old, she misbehaved at the dinner table while we were entertaining guests. So my husband, Floyd, escorted Peggy to her bedroom. As he was closing the door to her room, Floyd said, "When you're sorry, Peggy, you can come out."

Sometimes we only forgive enough to keep an open door, but we don't put the ax to the root of unforgiveness.

A few minutes later the door opened, but Peggy remained in her room. Floyd waited a little bit longer, but she didn't budge. Finally he went into her room and sat beside her on the bed. "Peggy," he asked, "are you sorry enough to come out now?"

She crossed her arms tightly across her chest and replied, "Nope! I'm only sorry enough to have the door open." Sometimes we, like Peggy, only forgive enough to keep an open door, but we don't put the ax to the root of unforgiveness.

Often the cause of a person's physical or emotional weakness can be traced to unforgiveness and unrepentance. This does not mean all suffering from ailments is because of unforgiveness. But forgiveness and repentance can release the healing power of God in you and in others.

Forgiveness, like confession, does not have to be an emotional experience. It is simply an "act of your will," responding to the Word of God by the prompting of the Holy Spirit.

Once you have forgiven others or God or yourself, know that the Lord is faithful and righteous to forgive you of your sin and cleanse you from all unrighteousness (see 1 John 1:9). Do not depend on your own understanding; trust the Lord, for His Word is true.

If your mind's attention is repeatedly drawn in a negative way to a person you have chosen to forgive, take authority over your thoughts. Command your mind, in Jesus' name, to dwell on thoughts that are true, honorable, right, pure, lovely, excellent and worthy of praise (see Phil. 4:8,9). Order the enemy to be silent, and cut off the power to your old memory circuits by refusing to listen to the devil's voice. Change direction by believing what God's Word says. It is helpful to quote Scripture verses aloud until you have the victory. You can also begin to thank the Lord for the positive qualities He has placed in that person and in the situation; pray God's blessing upon these positive areas.

Confession and Forgiveness Application:

Are you ready to be clean? Take time to allow the Holy Spirit to search your heart before God; ask Him to show you your heart. Don't search your own heart with your natural mind; you must perceive your own heart by the Holy Spirit. As you accept the Lord's cleansing and forgiveness, ask Him to refill you with the Holy Spirit.

The following are Scripture-based prayers of confession and forgiveness to help you when you pray:

Prayer of Confession

Father, I thank You for the blood of Jesus that cleanses me from all my sin. I come before You in the name of Jesus and ask to be restored to a right relationship with You and my brothers and sisters in Christ.

Father, Your Word says that if I confess my sin, You are faithful and just to forgive me and cleanse me from all unrighteousness. I come into Your presence to confess my sin of _____, knowing that I can draw near to You with a true heart in full assurance of faith, having my heart sprinkled from an evil conscience and my body washed with the pure water of Your Word.

Be gracious to me, Father. Blot out my transgression of _____. Wash me thoroughly from this iniquity and cleanse me from my sin. It is only against You, Lord, that I have sinned and done what is evil in Your sight. I ask Your forgiveness.

I now rejoice, not that I was made sorrowful, but that I was made sorrowful to the point of repentance. My repentance, according to Your will, leads me to eternal life in You. I receive Your abundant life where I was dead in sin. For the law of the Spirit of life in Christ Jesus has made me free from the law of sin and death. And whom the Son sets free shall be free indeed. Blotting out the handwriting of ordinances that were against me, which was contrary to me, You took it out of the way by taking it to Your Cross. I choose now to walk under this new covenant of liberty in Your Spirit life.

Father, I thank You that You have blotted out my sin(s), and as far as the east is from the west is how far You have removed them from me. I declare that this day my sin will be remembered no more, and if Satan brings it up again, he will have to deal with You.

(See 1 John 1:7,9; 5:6-9; Heb. 10:22; Pss. 51:1-4; 103:12; Col. 2:14; Rom. 4:7; 8:2; John 5:24; 8:32; 2 Cor. 3:6; 7:9-19; Ezek. 18:11; 33:16.)

Prayer of Forgiveness

Father, I come before Your throne with a heavy heart because (person or persons) has offended me and I have unforgiveness. I know unforgiveness is contrary to Your Word. Because of this, I have been tormented in my mind and emotions. This has created a binding tie between me and (person or persons).

Therefore, I ask, Father, that You forgive my sins of _____ , and I also forgive (person or persons) as You have forgiven me. I repent and let go of all bitterness, wrath, anger, clamor, slander, animosity and malice. I receive my forgiveness in Jesus' name and by His precious blood.

Thank You, Father, for setting (person or persons) and me free from all mental and emotional torment. I will not give the devil an opportunity. I will guard my mouth and let no unwholesome word come forth concerning (person or persons). I will speak words of life, power, health and healing. I will not grieve the Holy Spirit. I will be kind, tenderhearted, forgiving other people as You have forgiven me. I will not return evil for evil, or insult for insult, but I will speak words of blessing upon (person or persons).

I will walk in a manner worthy of You, Lord. I will determine to please You in all my actions and thoughts. I will bear fruit in every good work because I am a doer of Your Word and not a hearer only.

In Jesus' name, I command freedom to my body, soul, spirit, family and finances, because I am no longer under the curse of the law but have received my liberty.

I ask that the Holy Spirit rule in my life, bearing fruit to please You. Today I put off my old nature and put on Your love, joy, peace, patience, kindness, goodness, faithfulness, gentleness and self-control.

By a choice of my will, I make a fresh commitment to You, Lord, that I will live in peace with the saints and with my friends, coworkers, neighbors and family.

(See Isa. 59:1,2; Mark 11:25; Matt. 6:12,14,15; 18:21-35; 1 Pet. 2:1,2; 1 John 1:6,7; Eph. 4:25-32; 1 Pet. 3:8-12; Col. 1:10; 3:10; Jas. 1:22,25; Gal. 3:13,14; 5:22,23; Rom. 12:10,16-18; Phil. 2:2.)

Intercession

Jesus, your great high priest, provided the example of how to intercede when He was on earth, and assured you that He continues to intercede even now in heaven (see Heb. 7:25). Therefore, when you intercede, you are following His example.

The Bible tells you to intercede, and explains why in 1 Timothy 2:

First of all, then, I urge that entreaties and prayers, petitions and thanksgivings, be made on behalf of all men, for kings and all who are in authority, in order that we may lead a tranquil and quiet life in all godliness and dignity. This is good and acceptable in the sight of God our Savior (vv. 1-3).

The initiative for intercession comes from God! As an intercessor, you must be sensitive and responsive to the direction of prayer the Holy Spirit places on your heart. When Abraham was interceding for the city of Sodom, God said, "Shall I hide from Abraham what I am about to do?" (Gen. 18:17). Abraham was trying to save the whole city, not just Lot and his family. God communed with Abraham as a friend.

Intercession has been described as a love response to the prompting of the Holy Spirit for an urgent need. It can be a very simple cry to the Lord for someone you love. All His children are called to participate in this kind of prayer. In Galatians 6:2 we read, "Bear one another's burdens, and thus fulfill the law of Christ." God is pleased when you are a burden-bearer for others, coming in intercession on their behalf.

Daniel 10 records an instance when Daniel received a message from God concerning a great conflict between the angelic hosts. The Hebrew word translated "message" is sometimes translated "burden." Often when God gives you a message or a word, there is a heaviness or a burden placed upon you to pray that word into action. Sometimes the directive will be to pray the Word of God. At other times you may be led to do warfare against the enemy forces. Sometimes intercession may cause an anguish of heart, or a wrestling within your spirit.

You must be available to receive a prayer message or prayer burden from God. And when the Lord reveals His secrets to you in this way, it is a holy trust; do not take the matter lightly. If you feel the power of the Holy Spirit moving within your heart, be obedient to cry out to God on behalf of a spiritual leader, a nation or an individual as the Spirit brings names and places to your mind. Effective prayer requires availability, sensitivity and obedience.

Another admonition to intercede is found in 2 Chronicles 7:13-15:

If...My people who are called by My name humble themselves and pray, and seek My face and turn from their wicked
ways, then I will hear from heaven, will forgive their sin, and
will heal their land. Now My eyes shall be open and My ears
attentive to the prayer offered in this place.

How do you know what to pray for? The Scriptures give you
guidelines, and the Holy Spirit brings to you the most urgent
requests.

Make me know Thy ways, O Lord; teach me Thy paths.
Lead me in Thy truth and teach me, for Thou art the God
of my salvation; for Thee I wait all the day (Ps. 25:4,5).

The secret of the Lord is for those who fear Him, and He
will make them know His covenant (Ps. 25:14).

Begin by asking:

- Lord, what do You want me to pray for this person
  today?
- What is on Your heart?
- What is the most pressing need?
- How do You want me to intercede?

You may wonder, *How will I know if the Holy Spirit is calling me to
pray?* The Holy Spirit will show you by words, messages or
thoughts that stir your spirit. Sometimes these stirrings will
totally surprise you. (See "Hearing God's Voice," chapter 4.)
The following are ways to identify a call to pray:

- The Holy Spirit brings to mind a face, a name, a family,
  a church, a situation, a nation or a scene.
- God places a practical need upon your heart; perhaps
  one you have observed or heard expressed in everyday
  conversation. (Examples: A friend calls requesting
  prayer; the news media alerts you to a current event;
  you can't get someone off your mind, etc.)

- Something you witness—such as a car accident, a passing ambulance, a person in obvious need, someone being abused, or a crime taking place—prompts you to pray.

Remember, intercession generally begins and is ended by God. After He gives you a subject or topic to pray about, continue to pray until you feel He wants you to move on to something else. Continue to follow His leading.

Don't be surprised if occasionally you experience something unusual or unexpected, such as laughter, groans, weeping or travailing sounds. Paul admittedly prayed this way, saying, "My little children, of whom I travail in birth again until Christ be formed in you" (Gal. 4:19, *KJV*). Though the emphasis is not on a travailing type of prayer, it does sometimes accompany deep intercession. Many times you may pray in a very authoritative manner over the principalities and powers of the evil, unseen world. The Holy Spirit will set the tone.

When the burden for prayer is lifted, you may experience other emotions, such as peace, joy accompanied with laughter, or tears. Regardless of your feelings, know that your petitions have touched the Father's heart.

Petition

Petition is humbly making a formal request or supplication (to beg or beseech) to one in authority. When petitioning, you are asking the Lord for a specific grant or benefit, earnestly entreating Him for grace, mercy and favor toward a particular need.

How do you petition the Lord?
- You are to come to the Lord in childlike faith with your specific requests, knowing how much He desires to give good gifts to His children (see Matt. 7:11; Luke 18:17; Jas. 4:3).

What are the conditions for asking?
- Make sure your petition is properly motivated and that

it will glorify the Lord (see John 14:13; Jas. 4:2,3). Do not ask out of sheer selfishness.

- Ask in faith without doubting. Asking plus believing equals receiving (see Matt. 21:21,22; Mark 11:23; Heb. 3:12; Jas. 1:6).
- Ask in accordance with His will; His Word must be inside your heart (see John 15:7; Rom. 10:8-10; 1 John 3:18-22; 5:14,15).
- Abide in the true vine—Jesus. Abiding is a two-way commitment. You must hear, believe and do His Word; then the Father, Son and Holy Spirit will make their abode in you (see John 14:23; 15:1-10).
- Bear good fruit; it must also be lasting. His disciples prove to be good fruit bearers (see Matt. 7:15-27; 15:13; Luke 3:8,9; 8:14,15; John 15:2,16; Jude 12,13).
- Ask in the name of Jesus. He has given you the authority to use His name. His name has power on earth and in heaven and hell. Everything has to bow to His name (see John 14:13; 16:23b-24; Phil. 2:9,10).

What should I ask for?

- Whatsoever things you desire (see Mark 11:24; John 14:14; Phil. 4:6.).

When the Holy Spirit places a need or desire upon your heart, agree with Him, yield your will to His and begin to make your requests known to the Lord. As you pray and petition the Lord, He will birth a vision (mental impression) within your heart. This vision will always be in line with God's Word. It must not be otherwise! (See "Hearing God's Voice," chapter 4.)

Petitions must be specific requests! Hannah, the mother of Samuel, wanted a baby with all her heart, so she petitioned God for a child. Not only did Hannah petition God for a child, but she also asked specifically for a son, making an unselfish vow to give him back to God for service unto the Lord. The Lord heard her petition, granted her request, and Hannah bore a son; then she was obedient to fulfill her vow. Hannah had lived with her need for a long time; but when she expressed that need aloud, petitioning the Lord specifically, with a pure heart, she received exactly what she asked for (see 1 Sam. 1—2).

The following are other examples of petitions:

- Jacob prayed for safety (see Gen. 32:9-12).
- King Hezekiah asked God to spare his life (see 2 Kings 20:1-11).
- Abraham's servant prayed for success in his task of finding a wife for Isaac (see Gen. 24:12-14).
- The blind man cried out to Jesus to regain his sight (see Mark 10:51).

God wants you to petition Him—to ask, to seek, to knock. He has promised that if you ask, you will receive (see Matt. 7:7,8). "And this is the confidence which we have before Him, that, if we ask anything according to His will, He hears us. And if we know that He hears us in whatever we ask, we know that we have the requests [petitions] which we have asked from Him" (1 John 5:14,15). It is the Lord's pleasure to answer prayer. It glorifies Him to fulfill your request (John 14:13). But He wants you to do your part—to ask, to petition and to be specific in prayer.

Unanswered Prayers

I am frequently asked, "Why did my prayer go unanswered?" Quite often that means, "Why wasn't my prayer answered the way I wanted it?" or "I know God can, but why hasn't He?"

We do not have all the reasons for unanswered prayer, but we do have some of them based on the Word of God. In this section I will concentrate on 10 reasons. Often a negative statement can result in a positive answer, which is the method being used here:

1. *Not fellowshiping with God.* Every believer is called to fellowship with God, according to 1 Corinthians 1:9.

"Fellowship" means "to have companionship, partnership, communion; to simply spend time with." A "call" means "a summons, a request or an invitation." Jesus modeled this call to fellowship by going to the mountain to pray all night, especially when making major decisions (see Luke 6:12,13).

2. *Not praying to the Father in Jesus' name.* Jesus instructed His disciples to pray in His name, a directive that is as appropriate today as it was when He first spoke it (see John 15:16). This is a simple truth, but one that not all Christians follow.

3. *Not asking, or asking with wrong motives.* Some people believe God is too busy to hear their little prayers. But He says that whatever you ask, He hears. God wants more than your grocery list. He wants to dine with you. These truths are summed up in James 4:2,3 and Revelation 3:20.

4. *Not asking according to God's will.* God's will is learned by reading and hearing the Word of God, and spending time with Him. Salvation, for example, is explicit in God's Word. Men of God in the Bible knew His will when they prayed. Moses in Exodus 32:11-14 is a good example. Also read 1 John 5:14,15.

5. *Not having God's Word in you.* Jesus said in John 15:7, "If you abide in Me, and My words abide in you, ask whatever you wish, and it shall be done for you." Listening to the Bible on cassette tape is an excellent way to memorize His Word, even playing it all night alongside your bed.

6. *Doubt and unbelief.* James 1:5-8 tells you to ask God in faith without doubting. Jesus instructed His followers to believe for what they prayed so they would receive. Elijah the prophet, a man with a nature like ours, won great victories when he prayed (see 1 Kings 18), then ran from one woman when doubt set in (see 1 Kings 19).

7. *Losing heart or giving up.* Many prayers are not answered affirmatively because someone loses heart or gives up.

TYPES OF PRAYER   63

This is best expressed in Luke 18:1 (*Amp.*) when Jesus says that we "ought always to pray and not to turn coward (faint, lose heart, give up)." In the verses following that chapter, the widow received because she kept asking.

8. *Not being in agreement.* Jesus spoke on agreement in Matthew 18:19: "Again I say to you, that if two of you agree on earth about anything that they may ask, it shall be done for them by My Father who is in heaven." The marriage agreement is the strongest on earth. Strife and contention are contrary to agreement and will hinder prayers.

9. *Unforgiveness.* One of the strongest statements by Jesus follows what is commonly called The Lord's Prayer. In Matthew 6:14,15 He says, "For if you forgive men for their transgressions, your heavenly Father will also forgive you. But if you do not forgive men, then your Father will not forgive your transgressions." And did Jesus mean 490 times in Matthew 18:21,22? Consistent forgiveness means you wipe the slate clean and begin again at the count of one. God will not remember your sins when forgiveness is asked (see Isa. 43:25).

10. *Not giving tithes and offerings.* Tithing was required in the Old Testament, and the principle of giving abundantly can be found in the New Testament—the early believers were willing to give all (see Acts 2:44-47 and 4:32-37). Jesus had much to say about giving, and the blessings that come from giving. I'm often asked, "Do we give off the gross or the net?" The answer is simple: Do you want a gross or a net blessing?

In conclusion, the following are more reasons that prayers go unanswered, which if they apply, you may want to study further:

- Disobedience (see Deut. 1:42-45; Isa. 1:19,20; Heb. 4:6);
- Prejudice and hate (see Prov. 26:24-28; 1 John 2:9-12; 3:15-22);
- Unrepented sin (see Pss. 19:12,13; 66:18; Isa. 59:1,2);

- Overindulgence or not caring for your body, which is God's temple (see Prov. 23:1-8; Luke 21:34; 1 Cor. 3:16);
- Touching (attacking) God's anointed (see 1 Sam. 26:5-11; Ps. 105:15);
- Fear (see Ps. 56:4,11; Prov. 29:25; 1 John 4:18);
- Not examining yourself before communion (see 1 Cor. 11:27-31);
- Despising God's Word (see Prov. 28:9);
- Indifference (see Prov. 1:24-28);
- Neglect of mercy (see Prov. 21:13);
- Not honoring one another (see Deut. 5:16; 1 Pet. 3:7);
- Idolatry, which is anything you worship above God (see Deut. 7:25,26; Josh. 7; Ezek. 14:3);
- Speaking evil of brethren (see Gal. 5:26; Jas. 4:11; 5:9).

Section II

Hearing
from God

4

Hearing God's Voice

Draw near to God and
He will draw near to you.

—*James 4:8*

Communication is the life-giving blood that sustains all relation-ships. Without blood, the body dies; without communication, relationships die. When we communicate, we listen with our hearts to the one who is speaking and then respond. To know and recognize a person's voice, you must spend time with that person.

After 43 years of marriage, I have spent so much time with Floyd that I can usually read his body language before he opens his mouth to speak. I know Floyd's voice; I also know his ways. For example, when Floyd is going to broach a serious subject with me, he swallows three times. When he's irritated, my name is stretched over a long Texan pause...Beetthhhhh—this prepares me for what's coming next. I can identify his footsteps before he even enters the room. And the way he fluffs his pillow at night tells me we need to talk. Yes, I know Floyd.

Similarly, we can know God. We know Him through the per-son of the Holy Spirit. We learn His voice by spending time in prayer, and we learn His ways by studying His Word. We are never too young or too old to know God.

When my grandson Christopher was small, I would spend time talking to him about the Holy Spirit and how the Holy Spirit lives within him. One day after returning from a trip to Germany, I picked up Christopher and took him with me to run some errands. When we arrived at my office, the secretary gave him some chewing gum; then we stopped at the travel agency, and the travel agent gave him some candy. As we crossed the parking lot, I noticed his little cheeks were so stuffed with goodies that he looked like a chipmunk storing up for winter.

It was a scorching summer day and the Texas sun had turned my borrowed car into a slow baking oven. As I began to fasten Christopher into his seat, I realized that not only had all the candy been consumed, but all evidence of the gum had also disappeared. I thought *Oh no, I hope he didn't leave that gum on the seat of my dear friend's new car!*

I asked, "Christopher, what happened to your chewing gum?"

He replied, "You know."

To which I responded, "No, I don't know."

He insisted again, "Yes, you know, Nonnie."

And again I responded, "No, Christopher, I don't know. What did you do with that gum?"

"I swallowed it!" he exclaimed.

"Why did you do that?" I asked.

He innocently explained, "You see, Nonnie, Jesus lives inside of me and He wanted to chew it for a while. You know, Nonnie, sometimes He talks, sometimes He sings, and sometimes He just wants to chew gum!"

God Is Not a Silent Friend

God wants to speak to you personally; He wants you to hear His voice (see John 10:3-5). Drawing near to the Lord opens the door for Him to fellowship and communicate with you. His desire is to teach you (see Ps. 32:8), lead you into the truth, and show you things to come (see John 16:13-15).

The Lord speaks to you through the person of the Holy Spirit (see Ezek. 36:27; John 14:16,17). Jesus calls Him the Counselor (see Isa. 9:6; John 14:16,17; 2 Tim. 3:16). The word "counselor" comes from the Greek word *parakletos*, which literally means "one called alongside to help." It also means "comforter, strengthener, helper, advisor, advocate, intercessor, ally and friend." You need not be afraid to trust the voice of the Holy Spirit; He never moves outside of the character of the Lord and is always in harmony with the Word of God. He is your friend who is called to walk beside you and communicate with you. His is not a silent friendship (see Pss. 28:1; 37:3; John 12:49; 14:26).

God leads; Satan drives. God convicts;
Satan condemns and brings guilt.
God woos; Satan tugs hard.

God wants to instruct you and give answers to your questions (see Pss. 21:2; 119:169). You cannot depend on another person to hear Him for you. Hearing the Lord's voice becomes an everyday occurrence as you willingly spend time with Him and study His Word by meditating upon and memorizing Scripture (see Josh. 1:8; Ps. 119:11,16). Then when you hear His voice, you know that it is the Lord because it is in agreement with the Word of God. The more you know His Word, the more you will also understand His character and His ways (see Exod. 33:13; Pss. 25:4; 103:7).

One test to determine whether you are hearing the Holy Spirit is to ask: Is the voice gently leading, or is it commanding and harsh? God's voice gently guides and encourages, giving hope (see Ps. 18:35; Isa. 40:11; Jas. 3:17). God leads; Satan drives (see John 10:4,10). God convicts; Satan condemns and brings guilt (see John 16:8-11; Rev. 12:10). God woos; Satan tugs hard. When God speaks,

He does not use fear to motivate. If fear overcomes you, it is the enemy speaking, not God (see 2 Tim. 1:7).

Proverbs 4:20,21 says, "My son [or daughter], give attention to my words; incline your ear to my sayings. Do not let them depart from your sight; keep them in the midst of your heart."

Listening: A Key Part of Intercession

Many times you and I don't hear God's directive because we have not inclined our ear to Him. The prerequisite to hearing is listening! Often we are so busy talking ourselves that we can't possibly hear Him. And yet, He wants us to be so attuned to His voice that we can even hear Him in the midst of a crowd. Someone has said that we have one mouth and two ears because we need to listen twice as much as we speak.

And as we listen, we find that God's tone of voice changes just like ours does. Sometimes the Lord speaks with a loud thunder; other times He speaks in a still small voice. The Word commands us to keep on the alert; keep watching and waiting. When He calls us to intercede for someone, the Holy Spirit will reveal strongholds, special burdens, battle plans of the enemy, actions to take and prayer strategies. We must learn to identify His voice and to be sensitive to responding quickly. Remember, listening gets better as intimacy deepens. And know that even close relationships have times of silence.

When God is silent, keep waiting in faith and do not allow the enemy to cause you to succumb to unbelief (see Heb. 4:11; 1 Pet. 4:18,19). Focus on God's faithfulness and other positive attributes while you are waiting (Pss. 33:18; 36:5; 37:7,34; 143:1; Lam. 3:25,26; Phil. 4:8).

God's people needn't think that listening to Him is something difficult or only for the very "spiritual" or "mature." Even in the early months of infancy, a child learns to recognize the voice of the one who cares for it. The more time you spend with the Lord in total trust, just like a child, the more clearly you will recognize His voice. The ability to communicate increases with matu-

HEARING GOD'S VOICE   71

rity. You need to make time to listen to the King of kings, concentrating on what He is saying.

Jesus gave you His word that His sheep will hear His voice (see John 10:27). You are one of His sheep, and as long as you are part of the fold, you WILL hear His voice:

He who is of God hears the words of God (John 8:47).

How Does God Speak?

"God spoke to me" is one of the most misunderstood phrases among His people; it can create an atmosphere of misunderstanding, confusion, hurt, rejection, jealousy, pride and other negative responses. Perhaps you have run into someone who feels he or she has an edge on hearing from God and that everyone must accept what he or she is saying. If you are unfamiliar with the phrase "God told me," or you do not understand how to hear God's voice, you might feel inferior, thinking God never speaks to you.

First, understand that God RARELY speaks in an audible voice. This can happen, but it is not the normal way in which God speaks to people. God is Spirit and communicates with you through His Holy Spirit within you. John 14 says:

"And I will ask the Father, and He will give you another Helper, that He may be with you forever; that is the Spirit of truth, whom the world cannot receive, because it does not behold Him or know Him, but you know Him because He abides with you, and will be in you. In that day you shall know that I am in My Father, and you in Me, and I in you....If anyone loves Me, he will keep My word; and My Father will love him, and We will come to him, and make Our abode in him (you). But the Helper, the Holy Spirit, whom the Father will send in My name, He will teach you all things, and bring to your remembrance all that I have said to you" (vv. 16,17,20,23,26).

The Theater of Your Mind

You may be wondering, *If God does not speak audibly, how does He speak?* He speaks through the Holy Spirit in the theater of your mind and through spiritual hearing—in the same way you use your natural mind and hearing.

You do not think in words; you think in pictures. Imagine a friend saying to you, "You should have seen Tom (your best friend) on the street corner yesterday with his little girl. They were sharing about Jesus, and his daughter sang 'Jesus Loves Me' in such a special way." As you were being told, you could see Tom and his little girl sharing and singing. You could picture it in the theater of your mind and hear it with your inner ear because you know them both so well.

If you had just become engaged and wanted to tell your family, you would probably rehearse the situation again and again in the theater of your mind, seeing and hearing everyone's reaction.

Suppose someone talking to you said the word "man," then "woman," then "house." In the theater of your mind, you would not see the letters m-a-n, etc. You would see an impression of a man, woman or house. Now let's change those same words to "my father," "my mother" and "my house." These words bring a totally different impression to your mind. Who do you love most in the whole world? Now the picture is entirely different. Think back to a memorable experience that you and your favorite person shared. You do not see words, but rather an actual experience which has been indelibly imprinted upon your mind; you can hear and see what was said and done. You do not actually hear or see, but because this person is so special to you and the experience so profound, you can relive it again and again.

It is the same with the Lord. When you begin to spend time with Him and meditate on His Word, you, too, will see and hear Him and know Him, even better than the person you love most in the world. Time set apart for the Lord naturally develops into an intimate, loving relationship between you and Jesus. You have probably heard His voice many times, and undoubtedly the

Holy Spirit has given you impressions or pictures which you did not realize were from Him. Often men refer to the Holy Spirit's impressions as a "gut feeling" and women call it "a deep inner sense or inner knowing." I cannot overemphasize the fact that the Holy Spirit NEVER speaks to you contrary to the Word.

Testing the Spoken Word

If you receive a word and you are not sure whether it came from God, self or the enemy, first, search the Scripture to see what the Bible has to say about it. You might want to start with a good concordance and look up the words or word pictures as you receive them.

Let's consider the example of my call to prayer. I heard, "Elizabeth, I have need of you." I began to meditate on each word the Lord spoke.

Obviously, I knew my own name, and the word "I" meant THE LORD, the I AM. "Have" means *now*, or it could mean *in the future*. But what did Jesus have need of? Going to the concordance, I looked up "need." There I found that Jesus had need of only one thing—a donkey.

What then? I went to an encyclopedia and read about a donkey. The encyclopedia said that a donkey is a burden bearer that carries a weight many times greater than its size. Sometimes it carries the man; sometimes it carries the man's burden. And often it walks alongside the man.

Was the Lord calling me into intercession to help carry a man or a man's burden? (It was some time before this was confirmed and I realized God was calling me to carry both the man and the burden at various times in prayer.)

Guidelines for Hearing the Voice of God

Satan does not want you to hear God's voice because your partnership with the Lord can wreak havoc on his kingdom. Knowing that you will have to fight the enemy as you enter into your time alone with God will help you to stay true to your commitment. The following guidelines are tools to help you win the battle:

- **Bind the voice of the enemy.** When you pray, Satan will try to interfere. So before you start to pray, bind his voice. Do this in the name of Jesus. Then trust the Holy Spirit. He will lead you and guide you into ALL truth. (See Matt. 16:19; John 14:26; 15:26,27; 16:13-15; Jas. 4:7,8; 1 Pet. 5:8,9.)

- **Submit your own will and reasoning to the Holy Spirit.** Many times your own will and reasoning get in the way of what the Spirit of the Lord wants to share with you or communicate to you. Trust in the Lord with all your heart and lean not on your own understanding. (See Ps. 119:104,125; Prov. 3:5; 16:3; 1 Cor. 2:14-16; Jas. 4:7,8.)

- **Turn off your own problems.** This isn't always easy, but it is necessary to true communication. Concentrating on your own problems forms a "static" that can interfere and bring confusion, causing a mixture of interpretation. (See Pss. 37:5; 42:5; 43:5; Prov. 3:5; 14:30; Isa. 26:3; Phil. 2:4; 4:6,7; 1 Pet. 5:7.)

- **Give your undivided attention to God's Word.** Focus your mind on what He is saying; hearing is passive, while listening is active. This will require mental effort and attention. Satan will fight you on this because the more revelation of God's Word you have, the more of a threat you will be to the kingdom of darkness. (See Ps. 37:7; Prov. 4:4,20,23; 1 Cor. 2:10-12; 2 Cor. 10:5.)

- **Limit your own talking.** After you have petitioned the Lord, take time to be still and wait upon Him. You do this in the same way you would carry on a conversation with a precious friend. (See Num. 9:8; Pss. 18:28; 27:14; 31:24; 37:5; Song of Sol. 2:14.)

- **Write it down.** Listen to your inner thoughts and ideas. The Spirit of the Lord will speak to you through impressions or pictures in the theater of your mind.

When this happens, write them down, because with time there is a tendency to forget. And the Lord might want to add more later. Soon you will begin to see that what you have written fits into a pattern. As you continue to pray and see the answers to your prayers, certain pictures will take on a special meaning for you. (See Exod. 17:14; Pss. 16:7; 36:8b,9; 37:5; 77:6; Prov. 9:10; 16:3,9; 1 Cor. 2:9-16.)

- **Don't argue mentally.** When the Spirit of the Lord speaks, you may tend to argue with yourself and say, *That's just me, or my imagination.* But as you check your written notes, God will give you confirmation from previous times with Him, or He could be giving additional "witness" to His future plans. (See Isa. 46:10,11; John 16:13; 1 Cor. 2:16; 2 Cor. 13:1b; Phil. 2:5.)

- **Wait upon the Lord for the interpretation.** Don't try to figure out impressions when you receive them. Wait upon the timing and wisdom of the Lord. (See Pss. 27:14; 37:7; Prov. 2:6; 16:3; Dan. 2:22,23,28,30; John 10:4; Eph. 1:17; Col. 1:9.)

- **Don't get ahead of (or lag behind) the Holy Spirit.** Often when the Lord shows or tells us something, we get so excited that we run and share it; but the Spirit of the Lord isn't finished with us yet. Let Him develop the thoughts He gives you; wait until you know He is through. Don't try to make things happen. Proverbs 16:9 says, "The mind of man plans his way, but the Lord directs his steps." (See Jer. 10:23; 1 Cor. 4:5a; 2 Cor. 4:6; 2 Pet. 3:9a.)

- **Be trustworthy.** The Lord will share with you just as you share with a friend. He expects the same from you that you expect out of the one with whom you share your personal confidences. The more He can trust you with deep and intimate things, the more He will entrust to you. (See Gen. 18:17-19; Num. 12:7,8 Ps. 25:14; Isa. 45:3.)

- **The Holy Spirit speaks through music.** There are times in the mornings when you wake up with a song on your heart, such as "Only Believe." Listen to the words; during the day it could be the very key you will need to build your faith and lead you to victory. (See Exod. 15:1; 2 Chron. 20:21,22; Pss. 32:7b; 40:3; 42:8; 138:5; Eph. 5:19; Col. 3:16.)

- **Pay attention to your dreams.** The Lord often speaks in dreams and visions (word pictures). Eventually these dreams will fit into a pattern, and certain pictures or circumstances will begin to mean something which will help you to interpret what you have dreamed. Not all dreams are of God; those that are will stand out and will leave a deeper impression on you. You will be able to remember them beyond just waking up in the morning. Remember to write them down; this is the only way you will be able to recall the details. Even if you don't understand the dream, write down what you think it means to you. (See "Journaling: Recording What You Hear," chapter 6.) (See Job 33:14-16; Dan. 2:19-23; 4:18; 7:1,2,7,13; 9:21,22; 10:14,21; Matt. 1:20; 2:13.)

- **Don't be afraid of silence.** Sometimes the Lord is silent. Don't become upset if you don't hear anything when you pray. Often the Holy Spirit just wants to worship the Lord. When you have your heart clean before Him, then there is nothing wrong. He just desires that you come and bask in His presence because you love Him and want to be with Him. Be still and know that He is God. (See Pss. 45:11; 46:10; 96:9; Song of Sol. 1:4; Isa. 12:2,3; 30:15; 50:10.)

The Holy Spirit is the One who leads us into God's truth. And when the Holy Spirit speaks, His voice is unique to each individual. Thus, the more you understand the Holy Spirit's personality through you and others, the more clearly you will be able to discern God's truth.

5

Understanding the Holy Spirit

Now there are varieties of gifts, but the same Spirit.
And there are varieties of ministries, and the same
Lord. And there are varieties of effects, but the same
God who works all things in all persons.

—*1 Corinthians 12:4-6*

The Holy Spirit's personality has many facets. He is a person, and just as you and I experience different emotions and express ourselves in diverse ways, so does the Holy Spirit. But He never moves outside of God's Word, or exalts or calls attention to the flesh.

When I was taught this truth in Bible school, I began to understand the personality of the Holy Spirit in a whole new way. I also began to understand why people have so many different responses during a worship service, a prayer group or any other meeting.

Have you ever been in a service where the power of the Holy Spirit was so present and sweet that you felt like everyone should just be still, reverencing the Lord? Then you turned to the person standing next to you and realized that he, instead, was full of joy and excitement. He just wanted to sing, clap or move about. And you wanted to say, "Shh, don't you know that the presence of the Lord is in this place?" He, on the other hand, didn't understand why you were so somber. Perhaps both of you thought the other was missing the move of the Spirit; however, the Holy Spirit was operating in a different facet through each of you.

Isn't this contrary to the character and harmony of the Lord? No! For example, men and women in the Church do not all look alike, dress alike, talk alike or act alike. Neither do they act or look the same every day; they change day to day. The same is true with the Spirit of the Lord in you. As you yield to Him, the Holy Spirit will choose to move through you as He desires.

The Facets of the Holy Spirit

Because the Holy Spirit is a person, He has many facets to His personality. We could spend the remainder of this book studying the numerous traits within His character; however, in this chapter we will explore only eight.

- **Convicting or pleading.** John 16:8,9 says that "He [the Holy Spirit], when He comes, will convict the world concerning sin, and righteousness, and judgment; concerning sin, because they do not believe in Me." It is this facet that draws a person to Jesus. The Holy Spirit keeps His finger on what is wrong until the issue is settled. He often operates this way in church services.

    Billy Graham reportedly told a group of ministers in Greensboro, North Carolina, when asked, What is the secret to your ministry? "If there is a secret to my ministry, it is not my secret, it is the secret of the Holy Spirit. There are two things that I rely on heavily—first is the convicting power of the Holy Spirit, and second, I say 'the Bible says.'"

    Conviction can be a beautiful thing, but it can also be

very painful. When the conviction of the Holy Spirit moves upon a person, many emotions are aroused. Don't interrupt when the Holy Spirit is dealing with someone; wait upon the timing of the Lord. Pray and lend yourself as an assistant to Him.

I've never met anyone with whom God is dealing who does not become obnoxious. Unfortunately that's when we often blow it because we react in a like manner.

- **Cleansing.** The censorial nature of the Holy Spirit is the holy cry (righteous indignation) within you that causes you to hate sin or to take authority over the devil. The Spirit of the Lord rises up within you and causes you to hate the sin that destroys the people of God. This is the facet of the Holy Spirit that Jesus operated in when He cleansed the Temple:

> And they came to Jerusalem. And He entered the temple and began to cast out those who were buying and selling in the temple, and overturned the tables of the moneychangers and the seats of those who were selling doves; and He would not permit anyone to carry goods through the temple. And He began to teach and say to them, "Is it not written, 'My house shall be called a house of prayer for all the nations'? But you have made it a robbers' den" (Mark 11:15-17).

Jesus was angry at the sin committed against the physical temple of God, not at the people. It is the same today, only now His children are the temple of the living God—one not made of stone. Today when the Lord desires to cleanse His temples (people), He moves through the cleansing power of the Holy Spirit.

Paul tells us in Ephesians 4:26,27 to "be angry, and yet do not sin; do not let the sun go down on your anger, and do not give the devil an opportunity."

When the Holy Spirit moves through you in such a way, you will experience God's anger through righteous indignation, and yet not sin against the Lord. This kind of anger does not give place to Satan; it has an exact opposite effect.

A well-known Bible teacher describes righteous indignation in this way: "It is the Holy cry of the inner man by the Holy Spirit whereby the Spirit of God and the spirit of man in union cry out against that which is immoral, sinful, unjust and destructive to God's kingdom and to the body, soul and spirit of man."

This facet of the Holy Spirit not only moves in righteous indignation against the sinful nature of others but also against that which is sinful in you. It can be painful when the Spirit of the Lord begins to deal with your own nature in those things that are not pleasing to Him. As you allow His Spirit to drive out that which is unholy and unrighteous within you, you too will experience His cleansing power and this facet of His personality.

• **Communion.** This facet of the Holy Spirit desires a time of communion and fellowship with you. Communion is the exchanging of ideas, opinions, thoughts or feelings. The word "communion" interchanges with the word "communicate." The Lord wants you to come into His presence: He wants to share with you what is in His heart, and to hear what is on yours. In John 17, Jesus prays what is known as the High Priestly prayer. He prays to the Father for us to have the communion and fellowship with each other that They shared:

> "I do not ask in behalf of these alone, but for those also who all believe in Me through their word; that they may all be one; even as Thou, Father, art in Me, and I in Thee" (vv. 20,21).

There are times when the Lord just wants to commune

with you. He does this through many avenues, such as prayer, praise, worship, meditation and the study of God's Word. And the more you commune with Him, the more you will know Him and the other facets of the Holy Spirit's personality.

- **Compassionate.** Compassion is a facet of the Lord that carries with it an inner emotion. In Greek "to have compassion" literally means to have the bowels yearn...a yearning deep within the intestine. This is more than just a sympathetic concern; it creates an identity deep within that brings about the miraculous.

  Every place in Scripture stating that Jesus was "filled with compassion" brings with it a demonstration of the power of God for miracles. Jesus had compassion for the hungry and fed them all; He healed the blind, raised the dead, cast out demons and cleansed the leper. Jesus was always touched by the Spirit of Compassion when He saw His people like sheep without a shepherd. (See Matt. 9:36; 14:14; 15:32; 20:34; Mark 1:41; 6:34; 8:2 and Luke 7:13.)

- **Counseling**. Jesus said it would be advantageous that He go away and that He send a Counselor (Helper) to lead you and guide you into all truth. The Holy Spirit will not speak on His own authority, but whatever He hears, He will speak (see John 16). The Holy Spirit will teach and instruct through you.

  A counselor not only gives advice but also exchanges opinions and ideas with you, helping you to reach a decision or set a direction. He is one called alongside to help.

  This facet of the Holy Spirit counsels you and speaks through you to help you counsel others. Have you ever been to lunch with someone who had a problem or need? You opened your mouth, and out came wisdom that even you marveled at. You were such a help to that person, you decided to meet the following week and talk again. But the next week the same wisdom and counsel were not there. What happened? The power of the Holy Spirit was present the first time, but the next week He did not come in the same way:

> But the Comforter (Counselor, Helper,
> Intercessor, Advocate, Strengthener, Standby),
> the Holy Spirit, Whom the Father will send in My
> name [in My place, to represent Me and act on My
> behalf], He will teach you all things. And He
> will cause you to recall (will remind you of,
> bring to your remembrance) everything I have told
> you (John 14:26, *Amp.*).

- **Commanding.** This is the preemptory facet of the Lord. His command terminates all debate or action. *Webster's Dictionary* says, "...implies authority, power to control, and to require obedience." In Greek it means "to appoint or place appropriately, to appoint over and to put in charge."

  Jesus was in a boat with His disciples, and a storm began to rage. His disciples became afraid and woke Jesus up because they thought they were perishing. Jesus *commanded* the storm to cease.

> And they [his disciples] came to Him and woke
> Him up, saying, "Master, Master, we are perishing!"
> And being aroused, He rebuked the wind and the
> surging waves, and they stopped, and it became
> calm. And He said to them, "Where is your faith?"
> And they were fearful and amazed, saying to one
> another, "Who then is this, that He commands
> even the winds and the water, and they obey Him?"
> (Luke 8:24,25).

When you issue a command in the power of the Spirit of the Lord, you have the authority. You don't have to ask for it or demand it; it is yours by virtue of the Spirit of God. You cannot issue a command and expect results unless the Spirit of the Lord so directs. Prayer is an important part of knowing the will of God. When Paul fasted, the Lord gave the instructions.

There are many places in the Word where the Spirit of the Lord spoke a command and others obeyed, both in the spirit world and in the natural. Jesus commanded the spirits to leave, while Paul commanded the people not to leave the ship when it appeared to be sinking.

- **Conquering.** This facet of the Holy Spirit is the overcoming power of the Lord, that which causes you to be victorious. It is also the joy, triumph and exultation that comes forth when you know a victory has been won.

> This is what the Lord gave David when he overcame Goliath. He knew who he was in the Lord, and he went forth to conquer without fear or doubt (see 1 Sam. 17).

> The joy of conquering was felt when Moses, Miriam and the children of Israel sang the song of deliverance when they overcame the Egyptians (see Exod. 15).

There are many examples in the Word of the conquering facet of the Holy Spirit. And this we know: We are more than conquerors in Him.

- **Concert.** When the Lord is moving in this facet, He moves through a melody within your heart. The dictionary describes a concert as: "An agreement of two or more in a design or plan; union formed by mutual communication of opinions and views; harmony."

In this facet the Lord will bring comfort, joy, peace, direction, guidance, etc. Songs have ministered comfort and victory in times of grief, such as the song, "It Is Well with My Soul." It might come in the form of a chorus, song, poetry or melody you are familiar with, or it could come "hot off the press" from the Lord. You will see this facet work in harmony with all the other facets of the Spirit in a special way (see Exod. 15:1; Pss. 32:7; 147:7; Acts 16:25; Jas. 5:13).

Now you will be able to appreciate the different responses you observe in Christian gatherings. It's exciting to watch the Spirit of the Lord move differently in and through one another. Follow the Lord's leading in your own heart and let Him move through each person as He wills.

Prove All Things

As you are learning to hear the Lord's voice, you must also learn to prove (test and examine) all things:

> But examine everything carefully; hold fast to that which is good (1 Thess. 5:21).

When you hear the voice of the Lord, don't rely on your feelings and opinions. What you hear must be in line with God's Word and His character. The Holy Spirit will never overrule what the Word of God has spoken and declared to be true.

The following are a few ways to prove or test what you receive, or what is being said to you by others. Remember, this a learning process. Distinguishing truth will become easier as you mature spiritually, and His Word and ways become real to you. This is by no means all inclusive but a simple guide to follow, and it may help to keep you from error.

- **Never look to man, but to Jesus.** Never look to another person or seek words or confirmation from that individual. Many times God will use someone to confirm what He has spoken, but it will come to you unsolicited. It will be given in a manner of humility, and the person giving it will not seek self-affirmation. (See Ps. 119:1.)

- **Never set a time limit.** God's time and your time are not the same. There are prophetic words in the Bible that have not yet been fulfilled, but because the Lord has spoken them, they will come to pass. When you receive something from the Lord, it will be in His timing, so don't give up. (See 1 Chron. 17:11,12; Eccles. 3:11; Isa. 2:2; 46:10,11; Acts 7:17; 11:28; Rev. 1:1.)

- **Always confirm anything you receive with the Word of God.** The Lord will never tell you anything outside the bounds of His Word. Even if what you hear is exactly what you are looking for and confirms what you thought the Lord said, if it doesn't agree with the Word of God, throw it away. It will only lead you into deception. (See 2 Tim. 3:16,17.)

- **Don't take Scriptures out of context.** Look at the total meaning to avoid hurting or deceiving yourself or others. Many times people not only take Scripture out of context, but they also use Scripture in part to "confirm" what they want or make it fit their situation or circumstance. God does use Scripture to confirm, but not out of context. You must learn to judge according to the whole of Scripture. Every jot and tittle is important. (See Matt. 5:18; 2 Pet. 1:20,21.)

- **What if the word you receive is in line with the Scriptures, but you don't understand it or have a witness to it?** Put it away, pray over it and let the Spirit of the Lord bring it to pass. Remember, the Lord knows the future, and that word might be exactly what you need to confirm a situation or just to let you know that you are exactly where the Lord wants you. Give it the test of time. One of the reasons for writing it down is that you will not have confusion and doubt in the days ahead.

- **Don't judge another's word.** Only God knows the thoughts and intents of a person's heart. Many times you do not know a situation or understand the depth of what a person might be going through. What means one thing to you might mean something entirely different to the person to whom it is given. (See Prov. 14:10; Rom. 14:4; 1 Cor. 2:11.)

- **Never let words or pictures bring you into confusion or fear.** When fear or confusion set in, it is not of the Lord. God is not a God of confusion, nor does He use fear tactics to control you. (See John 14:27; Rom. 14:17; 1 Cor. 14:33; 2 Cor. 2:11; 2 Tim. 1:7.)
- **Has God placed a condition on the word He gave you?** "I will do this...if you will do that." Many times God will give us promises, but we must first fulfill His conditions. (See Prov. 2:1-6; 4:4.)

Responding to the Voice of the Lord

After the Holy Spirit has revealed the heart of the Lord to you, respond with an appropriate reply—an acknowledgment, a thank-you, a shout of victory or an action. Response to God sharpens your ability to hear. Enter freely into conversation with Him, and obey the directions He gives you.

During intercession, try to pause and listen often. After each petition is prayed through, bless the Lord for the work being accomplished for the Kingdom because of your prayers.

Always close your prayer in an attitude of joy, gratitude or praise, sealing the work of the Holy Spirit. The Lord's Prayer opens and closes with praise, giving you a good example to follow.

Don't become frustrated, thinking you have to go through each procedure and response. The Holy Spirit will lead you and guide you each step of the way.

Prayer Pointers

The guidelines that follow are not intended to limit you in any way. Rather, they are to lay a basic foundation to start you in a direction of communicating and communing with the Lord.

The greatest need is not that you always have great revelation, or pray brilliant prayers, but that you be faithful to the call of prayer. As you are obedient, the Lord's power will begin to flow. Even though you may not understand all the specific answers that come forth, you will see an awakening and strengthening of the Body of Christ. (See Heb. 11:13,39.)

- Begin your prayer with what you know are the obvious facts. Pray the Word and the precious promises of the Word given to you as His child.
- Always let the Holy Spirit be in charge. Remember you are just a soldier in the Army of God. Jesus is your "Commander in Chief." Let the Holy Spirit set the facet or the burden. Do not rely on your own insight. (See Rom. 8:26.)
- Pray and sing with understanding in your native tongue; also pray and sing in the spirit. (See 1 Cor. 14:15.)
- Pray in faith, expecting divine intervention. Pray in confidence. (See 2 Cor. 4:18; Heb. 11:6; 1 John 5:14,15.)
- Take time to listen. It is an important part of communication and one of the keys to successful intercession. (See Matt. 7:24.)
- Keep praying until the answer comes. Before moving on, wait until the Holy Spirit assures you that the task is accomplished. (See Luke 11:5-10; 18:1-8.)
- Flexibility and speed of response are often critical to victory. The only obedience that impresses God is instant obedience. Delayed obedience is disobedience!
- Meditate on the Word—renew your mind. Make sure all sin is under the blood of Jesus and that you are not harboring unforgiveness in your heart. (See Josh. 1:8; Prov. 4:20-24; Heb. 10:22; 1 John 1:7,9.)

6

Journaling: Recording What You Hear

And the Lord gave me the two tablets of stone
written by the finger of God; and on them were all
the words which the Lord had spoken with you.

—*Deuteronomy 9:10*

The phrase "It is written" is found repeatedly in the Word. God, Himself, wrote the Ten Commandments. The role of the scribes was very valuable during Bible days for recording important events and for keeping track of earlier writings and genealogies. As we begin to hear God's voice, we, too, must establish the habit of journaling—maintaining a personal written record of experiences, observations, etc., on a regular basis.

Many people do not like journaling, and yet journaling is one of the most important disciplines of a Christian's life. The hardest part of journaling is cultivating the habit; but those who do, reap great benefits from it.

Where Do I Begin?

Journaling should always begin with the date of entry. As time goes by, you may forget when certain events happened. But your journal will help you to trace patterns that have occurred around different circumstances in your life.

Whenever God gives you something, write it down; record impressions, words or Scriptures you receive during your prayer time. This is not necessarily every day, but often. Your journal need not be fancy, but it should be confidential; it will often contain details you don't want anyone but God to read.

A friend sent me the following poem regarding her journal:

Now I lay me down to sleep...
I pray the Lord my soul to keep.
If I should die before I wake,
Throw my journal in the lake!

Sometimes it's good to share specific entries with others, but ask God before you do. There are times when God will show you something that is not to be shared; it's only to be prayed for. Make sure you hold His secrets in trust.

Back in the early '70s, I was praying one morning when God showed me a certain man. From the front, the man was white; from the back, the man was gray. I asked, "Lord, what does that mean?" At first I didn't receive anything. Then I got the word "deception." I wrote the word down and waited. Next I heard, "He will be one way to your face, but he is very undecided." Finally I saw him turn and he became gray and black. The Lord then said, "Because of the grayness in this man, he will gradually go into deception. Beware."

I recorded everything the Lord showed me that morning. When the time of reckoning came with this man, I realized that God had prepared me and that what I was seeing was more than just my imagination.

Why Journal?

It is difficult to trust to memory all the things you hear and receive—especially if you do not fully understand what the Lord is saying. Your journal isn't for God or others—it's for you.

The Lord may speak things to you that will actually come about days, months or years later. How many times have you said, "If I could just remember...," or "If I had only written it down...."

Keeping a journal increases your faith as you come to realize that you really do hear from the Lord, especially when the things you have written down begin to come to pass.

How to Journal

There are many different ways of keeping a journal. Your journal should *always* include any impression, Scripture or picture you receive while praying for a person or situation. You should record not only what you have seen and heard, but also your own feelings and interpretation at the time. Then when God answers, you can check your feelings or impressions with the outcome.

Be sure you record the date each time you make an entry.

Journals do not have to be expensive or fancy. Some people find a loose-leaf or spiral notebook adequate, or a daily log book. Others prefer to purchase a journal from a stationery store, or use a computer. Try several different ways before you find one that works best for you. What matters most is that you record your times with the Lord.

You might want to separate your journal into subjects that relate to you, such as family, church, business, friends, impressions, etc. Are you praying for a particular friend or family member? Put his or her picture at the top of the page, with your prayer requests under it and the answers as they come.

A dear friend of mine meets with God at the beginning of each year to ask for the names of those the Lord wants her to pray for. She then includes their pictures in her journal and asks the Lord for a specific verse to pray for each person. Every day she prays over the pictures and writes whatever impressions, words or Scriptures the Holy Spirit gives her throughout the year. It's a blessing to know that Floyd and I are part of her journal.

I have several personal prayer partners with whom I am very close. For years now, we have given each other a Scripture verse as a Christmas gift. This year, however, we drew names and have committed to keeping a journal for the person whose name we picked. At the end of the year we will exchange journals. I treasure this experience.

One of the ways that God often speaks to me is with pictures. Although I am certainly not an artist, I do sketch the pictures the Lord gives me. For example on April 18, 1982, I drew the following sketch in my journal:

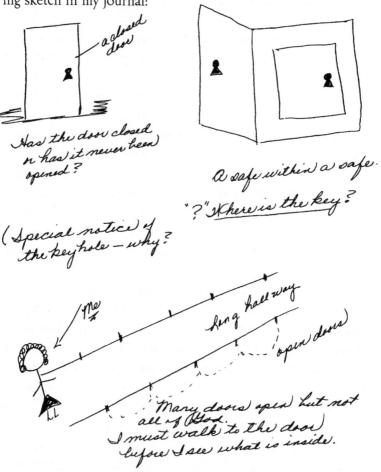

a closed door

Has the door closed or has it never been opened?

(Special notice of the keyhole — why?)

A safe within a safe. "?" Where is the key?

me

long hall way

open doors

Many doors open but not all of God. I must walk to the door before I see what is inside.

I saw a door and the door was closed. Immediately what came to mind is that when God shuts a door, no person can open it. Then

I asked the question, Was the door just closed or has it never been open? I really did not know. I also saw a safe within a safe. The door on the first safe was wide open; the door on the second safe was not. I noticed the keyholes, but I noticed the key was missing. Next I saw myself entering a long corridor with many doors on both sides (some open; others closed).

I knew I would not realize what was behind each door until I reached it. The Lord then spoke Revelation 3:8 into my mind, *Behold, I have put before you an open door which no one can shut.*

I asked the question, How will I know which door to choose? A Scripture immediately came to my mind, *A man's mind plans his way, but the Lord directs his steps and makes them sure* (Prov. 16:9, Amp.). I recorded every detail and put the word away, leaving it with God.

Later I was teaching in Germany and doing an exercise on hearing the voice of God when a man approached me with the following word and sketch:

"Beth, I see a door before you that was previously closed, but is now open. The date was December 12, 1984 (two years later). I see a safe and there's another safe inside that one which has been opened [This was just like the safe I had seen before]. Inside there is a map of Germany. Elizabeth, God is giving you a key to open something in all of my country. I saw a big key and it looked like this:

And I saw a large hallway with many open doors, but you did

not know what was behind the door until you reached it. What God opens no man can close—Revelation 3:8."

Ten years passed and I was teaching on hearing the voice of God in Sweden in 1994. Because I did not have an overhead projector to use, I began drawing a picture of the keyhole I had received in my sketch which was later confirmed in Germany. All

of a sudden, as though the Lord were whisking back a curtain, I received the revelation that the key was actually the logo for our ministry, Intercessors International. As I looked at the keyhole and then at our logo, I began to weep. God is faithful!

INTERCESSORS INTERNATIONAL

If I had not drawn the picture in my journal, I would have missed a great opportunity to see the Lord present, confirm and bring to pass His plans for my future. Journaling is a great blessing!

When you receive a picture in the theater of your mind, draw it out. It doesn't have to be fancy, just something to jog your memory when you look back over it. Label what or who each person or item might mean. Time can be your enemy when it comes to remembering details.

One of the reasons it is important to record visions is that shortly after we receive the picture, the enemy will try to put confusion on us. But when we have recorded it, we can overcome the enemy's tactics with "It is written."

I recommend writing out any Scriptures you receive, especially if you're a new Christian. This makes for a quicker reference when you look back to what the Lord spoke to you—it also helps you to commit the Word to memory.

Keeping a journal can be one of the most rewarding things you do for yourself. If you will be dedicated for 21 days, you will find you have established a habit pattern and the rewards will be phenomenal.

Section III

Spiritual
Warfare

Chapter 11

Spiritual
Warfare

7

You're in a Battle

For our struggle is not against flesh and blood,
but against the rulers, against the powers, against the
world forces of this darkness, against the spiritual
forces of wickedness in the heavenly places.

—*Ephesians 6:12*

Dutch evangelist Corrie ten Boom said, "It's a poor soldier indeed who does not recognize the enemy." The key to victory in both natural and spiritual warfare is to clearly identify the enemy, and to understand his character and methods.

Identify the Real Enemy

So who is the Christian's enemy? The answer is Satan and his host of fallen angels. Our opposition and struggle is against these unseen spiritual forces. (See Isa. 14:12-14; Eph. 6:12; 2 Pet. 2:4; Jude 6.)

Webster's Dictionary defines an enemy as a hostile force or power that has destructive effects. Several Hebrew words are translated "enemy" in the Old Testament. They can mean "enemy or foe; one who is awake; adversary or distresser; one standing against; one hating; observer or one who is critically watching."[1] The name Satan literally means "an adversary" or "one who accuses."[2]

According to author C. S. Lewis, "Satan's cleverest trick is to convince the world that he does not exist."[3] Few people, either Christian or non-Christian, have a clear concept of who Satan is and his place in the world. We succumb to our human reasoning in believing some person is our enemy—and act accordingly. Meanwhile, the real enemy, Satan, wreaks havoc in our marriages, families, churches, communities and nations.

Puritan pastor William Gurnall, in his book *The Christian in Complete Armour (Volume I)*, illustrates my point:

> Spend your wrath on Satan, who is your chief enemy. Men are only his puppets. They may be won to Christ's side and so become your friends at last. Anselm explains it in the following manner: "When the enemy comes riding up in battle, the valiant soldier is not angry with the horse, but with the horseman. He works to kill the rider so that he may possess the horse for his own use. Thus must we do with the wicked. We are not to bend our wrath against them, but against Satan who rides them and spurs them on. Let us pray fervently, as Christ did on the cross, that the devil will be dismounted and these miserable souls delivered from him."[4]

Satan was a perfect creature until he tried to exalt himself above God. His beauty filled him with pride—causing him to no longer be holy—and he wanted to receive worship that belonged only to God. Because Satan did not recognize the authority of God who made him, he was cast out of heaven, as recorded in the following passages:

> How you have fallen from heaven, O star of the morning, son of the dawn! You have been cut down to the earth, You who have weakened the nations! But you said in your heart, "I will ascend to heaven; I will raise my throne above the stars of God, and I will sit on the mount of assembly in the recesses of the north. I will ascend above the heights of the clouds; I will make myself like the Most High" (Isa. 14:12-14).

You were the anointed cherub who covers, and I placed you there. You were on the holy mountain of God; you walked in the midst of the stones of fire. You were blameless in your ways from the day you were created, until unrighteousness was found in you. By the abundance of your trade you were internally filled with violence, and you sinned; therefore, I have cast you as profane from the mountain of God. And I have destroyed you, O covering cherub, from the midst of the stones of fire (Ezek. 28:14-16).

After losing his residence in heaven, Satan was next seen in the Garden of Eden, where he deceived humanity (see Gen. 3:1-13), causing humans to rebel against their Creator and drawing the line of battle between the two kingdoms: the kingdom of Light and the kingdom of darkness.

As one Bible scholar states: "Satan is a creature; he is no match for the Creator. Satan is powerful, but not omnipotent. He can hinder, but he cannot prevent. The master of deceit can convince the prayer warrior that his or her prayer has not reached the Throne. Your strength is to remember that Satan is a defeated antagonist. To accredit it to him otherwise is to allow Satan supremacy over you. He is—and always will be—the Usurper. You cannot avoid warfare. You are continuously involved in the battle. Therefore, you must 'Draw near to God, resist the devil [stand your ground] and he will flee.'"

Know Your Enemy's Names

Let us examine some of Satan's names recorded in Scripture so you can better understand the character of your enemy. Many of his names not only reveal his character, but also suggest his tactics in warfare against the Body of Christ:

- devil
  (Matt. 4:1,5,8,11; 1 John 3:8,10; Jude 9; Rev. 12:9,12; 20:2);
- father of lies
  (John 8:44);

- god of this evil world
  (2 Cor. 4:4);
- an infidel or unbeliever
  (2 Cor. 6:15);
- prince of the bottomless pit or angel of the abyss
  (destroyer)
  (Rev. 9:11);
- angel of light
  (2 Cor. 11:14);
- star of the morning, son of the dawn
  (Isa. 14:12);
- the enemy or the avenger
  (Ps. 8:2);
- evil one
  (Matt. 6:13; John 17:15);
- adversary
  (1 Pet. 5:8);
- ruler of demons (Beelzebub)
  (Matt. 12:24);
- the destroyer
  (Job 15:21; 2 Thess. 2:3);
- the accuser
  (Rev. 12:10);
- the tempter
  (Gen. 3:1; Matt. 4:3; 1 Thess. 3:5);
- the dragon
  (Rev. 12:7-13; 20:2);
- the serpent
  (Gen. 3:1-4,13; Rev. 12:9; 20:2);
- the deceiver
  (Gen. 3:13; 2 John 7; 2 Thess. 2:3).

The Enemy's Tactics

As we see by Satan's names, his military might is camouflaged in blame, deceit and darkness. Satan's greatest strategy has been to convince the world that he does not exist. By perpetuating this lie, he is able to sneak up behind God's creation and whisper accusations that cause men and women to blame each other and their circumstances instead of himself. This has been an especially effective tactic against those who have joined the ranks of God's army. His little bombs of gossip and blame have so infiltrated the ranks of God's troops that Christian soldiers often fight each other instead of penetrating the enemy's camp to save the millions of hostages who are bound by his yoke of oppression and floundering in his hopeless den of darkness.

Satan beguiles us by convincing us that he has claim to the principalities (Christ referred to him as the prince of this world—see John 12:31; 14:30; Eph. 2:2). His rule is limited to:

1. this time, not the hereafter;
2. the world, not heaven;
3. the people in darkness, not the children of light.

He disarms and disables us by perpetuating spiritual sins that promote his kingdom and threaten to kill, rob and destroy our destinies. He deceptively lurks around masked as an angel of light, causing the Christian army to be off guard and fall prey to indifference, passivity and prayerlessness. When God's warriors awaken for momentary bouts of urgency, he convinces them to fight for trivial things, rather than for heaven itself.

How does he do this? He attacks your mind. When Satan can't get you to fall asleep at your battle station, he uses your mind to accuse you and judge you; then he keeps you in that position by guarding over you.

He raises doubt through suggestions such as, "You're not a Christian...look at what you did yesterday." And, "You aren't really saved; you can't give the exact date that you accepted Jesus." Or, "Look at you; you have a shameful past."

He creates fear: "These times you live in are hopeless." "What if you get cancer?"

He steals from you financially: You have car problems; the water heater breaks; your air conditioner goes out; you lose your job, etc.

Satan also uses your fear of man: "Everybody will laugh at me if I talk about Jesus." "What will people think if...?" When you become a God pleaser more than a man pleaser, one of your biggest battles is won.

Be Alert

You can win the daily battles with your enemy by recognizing that to fight Satan, you must fight in the realm of the spirit. Spiritual things are spiritually discerned, not figured out by human reasoning. You are not fighting flesh and blood, but the powers of darkness.

Be alert to cycles or patterns in attacks from the enemy—a rash of accidents and sicknesses that lead to death. DON'T FEAR. You have all authority and power in the name of Jesus. (See "Weapons of Warfare," section IV.)

You may wonder, *If Jesus won the battle, why are we still fighting?* Let's look at the end of World War II. Even though the victory was won and Hitler was defeated, occupation troops remained in different areas of the nations. In the same way, you must maintain the victory that was won at Calvary through the blood of Jesus.

Recognize the Battlefield

Scripture teaches that humans are tripartite beings, made up of spirit, soul and body:

> Now may the God of peace Himself sanctify you entirely; and may your spirit and soul and body be preserved complete, without blame at the coming of our Lord Jesus Christ (1 Thess. 5:23).

In the soulish realm—the seat of the intellect, emotions and will—the mind is our most common battleground, for it is in the mind that choices are made. These choices, all of which involve the will, determine not only the course of a person's daily life, but also his or her eternal destiny.

As the Word of God becomes alive in you and you act upon it, the Word will change your heart and mind, and your actions will change for your good and God's glory. Through Christ, the believer can receive revelation and understanding of spiritual mysteries, whereas the unbeliever is spiritually blind. (Compare Eph. 1:17-21 to 4:17,18.)

Scripture clearly teaches that Jesus has defeated Satan—stripped him of his power—and put all things under Christ's feet (see Eph. 1:19-22). The enemy's primary point of attack is against your mind, to raise questions—as he did in tempting Eve in the garden and Jesus in the wilderness—to influence you to doubt God's Word and His faithfulness.

Your mind has three voices to which it may respond: God's, the enemy's and your own. The more you become familiar with God's Word, the easier it will become for you to recognize God's voice; He always speaks that which is consistent with His character, as revealed in His Word. The voice of the Holy Spirit will speak to provide encouragement, comfort, direction, revelation, assurance of God's love, conviction or correction.

By contrast, the enemy usually speaks in a way that brings thoughts of doubt, guilt, fear, jealousy, hatred, self-condemnation or self-righteousness. Your own "self-talk" is usually based on your human logic and reasoning, or your selfish desires and will.

You must take authority over the voice of the enemy and forbid him to speak: "Submit therefore to God. Resist the devil and he will flee from you" (Jas. 4:7). Bind your own voice of human reasoning and desire; then open your mind and spirit to receive the voice of the Holy Spirit. Often the direction for prayer which the Holy Spirit gives does not seem logical to the human mind; do not allow this to hinder your obedience and effectiveness. When God calls you to take a stand, obey Him (see Isa. 55:8):

Blessing Follows Obedience

Blessing follows obedience as surely as night follows day,
And God rewards the man whose time is set apart to pray.
Rarely does the answer come from channels we would choose,
And often just before we win, it looks as though we'll lose.
But our God is faithful; His ways no man can understand—
He only asks obedience to stand when He says stand.

—*by Karen Kaufman*

Spiritual things must be spiritually discerned—not figured out by human reasoning. Affirm the truth of Paul's teaching: "I have the mind of Christ." (See 1 Cor. 2:14-16.)

Recognize that your fight is not with flesh and blood, but with the powers of darkness and Satan's spiritual rulers of this age. This age (world) has become the battleground between these satanic forces and humankind. Therefore, you are not fighting against people you know or with whom you come in contact in your daily life. The enemy may harass you by stirring up strife in the lives of people who are close to you in order to deter you from prayer and intercession. Always remember that the real battle is in the spiritual realm, and not in your physical circumstances.

Satan sends assignments against your spirit, soul and body. If he can keep you oppressed, he can keep you from growing spiritually and from being an effective intercessor. Taking authority over the enemy and making the right choices according to God's Word will bring you into victory and increase your spiritual growth. Failure to make the right choices gives ground to physical sickness, emotional problems and stunted spiritual growth.

Strategy for Warfare

The work of the intercessor is to combat the enemy in the spirit realm (as opposed to the natural realm), using spiritual weapons (not carnal ones). In the process, he or she must determine strategy for warfare through the guidance and revelation of the Holy Spirit. Discernment is a key element in your strategy, and a vital quality for leaders and intercessors to possess. "Discern" means "to distinguish or separate." God said to His prophet Jeremiah, "If you extract the precious from the worthless, you will become My spokesman" (Jer. 15:19).

Activity in the heavenlies is intensifying as the time of the Messiah's sure return draws near. Intercessors seem to be saying with one voice, "The conflict is real, and the battle lines are being drawn!" As spiritual warfare intensifies, particularly in the area of the mind, the intercessor's prayer life must not falter.

Satan doesn't fight fair in this battle. If he can't keep you from praying, he will assail you with doubt, discouragement and fear as you look at seemingly impossible circumstances. This deceiver will try to make you feel you are being objective and getting a lay of the land as you look at the situation. In reality his goal is to sideline you with an attitude of hopelessness and passivity.

You need to know your enemy! General Douglas McArthur, when stating some important requisites of military victory, gave the following:

- A will to win: a cause worth dying for.
- Strength: adequately trained and well-equipped personnel.
- Adequate source of supply: lifelines must be kept open.
- Knowledge of the enemy: "The greater the knowledge of the enemy, the greater the victory."

These same elements are necessary for maintaining your victory. Jesus has won the victory. It is your place to occupy until He comes.

Let's look at Nehemiah and see how he overcame the battle of the mind.

The Lord put the desire in Nehemiah's heart to rebuild the wall around Jerusalem. As he fasted and prayed over the situation, God gave him favor with the king. The king then released him to go back to his homeland to rebuild the city wall.

How did Satan fight that? By waging a battle in Nehemiah's mind. First, he attacked Nehemiah's reputation by trying to make a mockery of his efforts, saying, "Even what they are building—if a fox should jump on it, he would break their stone wall down!" (Neh. 4:3).

When mockery and discouragement failed to deter Nehemiah, the next tactic the enemy tried was intimidation and fright (see vv. 10-12). Nehemiah knew the enemy was trying to render him helpless through fear.

Then the enemy (in the form of two men) sent word, "Come, let us meet together at Chephirim in the plain of Ono" (6:2). With this Nehemiah recognized a major principle in warfare: "Never negotiate with the enemy!" Though this threatening message was sent to him FIVE times, Nehemiah steadfastly refused to negotiate on enemy territory.

This warrior builder also resisted the advice of a false prophet who tried to get him to run and hide from the enemy (see 6:12). He prayed from God's perspective, and fearlessly moved on to fulfill the commission God had given him.

Satan still tries to lure you into his encampment through the mind, just as he tried to do with Nehemiah. There is no mention of battle, only that which was done through the battle of the mind. You are defeated the moment you sink to the enemy's level.

Satan and his ruling spirits give specific assignments to the fallen angels—or demons—in his army. They will seek to manipulate circumstances and people in order to carry out their assignments. However, as a believer, you have the power and the authority to thwart their success and to destroy their assignments and curses. Not only that, but you can also turn those curses back upon the ranks of the enemy to do greater damage to Satan's cause than he intended for the body of believers. (See Acts 13:6-12.)

A study of Scripture indicates that Satan has delegated spiritual rulers to be in charge of countries and geographical areas. Read Ezekiel 28 and Daniel 9 and 10 for an example of how strongholds operate over a geographical area. Keep in mind that the spiritual warfare takes place in the heavenlies, but the effects of that warfare are seen upon the earth and in people's lives.

Consider the story of an evangelist in Latin America who was passing out tracts and witnessing to people on the streets of a particular city. A provincial boundary ran through the heart of the city. The evangelist met great opposition from the people with whom he tried to share the gospel; they threw the tracts in the gutter and refused to listen to his message.

The spiritual warfare takes place in the heavenlies, but the effects of that warfare are seen upon the earth and in people's lives.

In frustration, the evangelist crossed to the other side of the street, which was in a different province and under a different government. Suddenly he realized the attitude of the people on this side of the street was completely different—though their language and outward appearance was the same as the first group of people he had encountered. These people gladly accepted the gospel tracts, and eagerly listened to his message of salvation.

Sometime later the evangelist learned that a group of Christians in the second province had been binding the forces of darkness in their area, and praying for the gospel to go forth. Because of their spiritual warfare, the work of the evangelist was fruitful. But apparently no one was waging warfare on behalf of the first province, and resistance to the gospel was very strong.

In Daniel's experience, the "prince of the kingdom of Persia" withstood the angel whom God had sent with the answer to the prophet's prayers (see Dan. 10:12,13). When Daniel prayed, his prayers brought additional reinforcements into the spiritual conflict, and the prince of Persia was overcome. Daniel influenced the entire nation of Israel through his fasting and his persistent prayer.

Ask the Lord for specific revelation and discernment concerning the leaders for whom you are praying, and for the areas in which they are ministering. In praying for those who work among Muslims or in an area where cults are prevalent, you will be combatting an antichrist spirit. Where occult activity is strong, you are also dealing with spirits of deception, control and seduction (see 1 John 2:18).

In an area where there are many churches, but much conflict among the leaders and members, the Holy Spirit may reveal to you that the problem is a religious spirit ruling over that area, along with spirits of strife, contention and self-righteousness. Discerning the spirits responsible for a given problem—if indeed evil spirits are responsible—will make your intercession more specific and more effective.

It's important to discern patterns or cycles in attacks from the enemy. For some period of time there have been strong attacks against marriages among spiritual leaders. One particular denominational group has lost a large number of missionaries to cancer. Then there was a rash of serious accidents causing death or severe injury to ministers and missionaries, and/or their family members. The intercessors should serve as "watchmen on the wall" (see Isa. 62:6,7) to help ward off these attacks through spiritual warfare, and to lend their support by praying for those on the front lines of ministry.

Put On Your Spiritual Armor

Since you are engaged in a spiritual battle, it is wise to be acquainted with the armor of God which secures your safety and allows you to withstand the attacks of the enemy in these evil days:

Finally, be strong in the Lord, and in the strength of His might. Put on the full armor of God, that you may be able to stand firm against the schemes of the devil. For our struggle is not against flesh and blood, but against the rulers, against the powers, against the world forces of this darkness, against the spiritual forces of wickedness in the heavenly places. Therefore, take up the full armor of God, that you may be able to resist in the evil day, and having done everything, to stand firm. Stand firm therefore, having GIRDED YOUR LOINS WITH TRUTH, and HAVING PUT ON THE BREASTPLATE OF RIGHTEOUSNESS, and having shod YOUR FEET WITH THE PREPARATION OF THE GOSPEL OF PEACE; in addition to all, taking up the SHIELD OF FAITH with which you will be able to extinguish all the flaming missiles of the evil one. And take THE HELMET OF SALVATION, and the SWORD OF THE SPIRIT, which is the word of God. With all prayer and petition pray at all times in the Spirit, and with this in view, be on the alert with all perseverance and petition for all the saints (Eph. 6:10-18).

The armor described in Ephesians 6 is compared to that of a Roman soldier. A common complaint of the soldiers was that the armor was very heavy. Without proper exercise and discipline, the armor became weighty and would cause a soldier to lay it aside, leaving him undisciplined for battle and unprotected from the enemy.

Your spiritual armor fulfills the same function spiritually as the physical armor fulfilled for the Roman soldier. You are called to walk with Christ *daily*. You must be disciplined not only to put on the armor, but also to wield your weapons in battle against the forces of darkness. Your armor is to be a defense against the strategy of the devil to protect you from assault. The sword of the Spirit (God's Word) is an offensive weapon to attack, overpower and plunder the spoil of the powers of darkness. Lack of exercise and discipline will leave you open to assault. Therefore, be diligent as a soldier of God's army, always wearing your armor and ready for battle.

Keep in mind that the Roman soldier was expected to be in full-time service to his commanders. Paul makes reference to this in writing to Timothy:

No soldier in active service entangles himself in the affairs of everyday life, so that he may please the one who enlisted him as a soldier (2 Tim. 2:4).

This symbolizes the Christian's loyalty to Jesus Christ, the Commander in Chief, living a life of single-minded allegiance to Him.

Romans 13:12,14 says: "Let us therefore lay aside the deeds of darkness and put on the armor of light...put on the Lord Jesus Christ." Your spiritual armor is, in reality, the Lord Jesus Christ. He wants to be your defense by clothing you in Himself. You walk in total security when you walk daily covered in Jesus. Unlike conventional armor, your spiritual armor should never be taken off!

The following are reasons you need to daily put on the armor:

- It helps you to stand against the schemes of the devil.
- It keeps you strong in the Lord and in the power of His might.
- It enables you to resist in the evil day of the enemy's attack.
- It secures your safety and repels the enemy.
- It accomplishes the Father's will.

Walking in Triumph

With your armor of God in place, know that it is in and through Christ Jesus alone that you triumph.

But thanks be to God, who always leads us in His triumph in Christ, and manifests through us the sweet aroma of the knowledge of Him in every place. For we are a fragrance of Christ to God among those who are being saved and among those who are perishing (2 Cor. 2:14,15).

According to James M. Freeman, a Roman military procession of triumph was one of the spectacular events of ancient times. It was granted to a conqueror when he had met all the qualifications of victory established by the Roman Senate. One of these qualifications was that the victory be complete and decisive, putting an end to war. In this victory NO enemy could remain.

On the day chosen for the triumphal procession, people crowded into the streets and onto buildings to get a good view of the conqueror in whose honor it was held. This procession was made up of the conqueror, the senate members, heads of state, chief citizens and the prisoners who had been captured. The valuable spoils of the war were prominently displayed.

The conqueror, wearing a robe embroidered with gold and a tunic covered with flowers, rode in a special chariot drawn by four horses. In his right hand he held a laurel wreath which was the symbol of the crown of a conqueror; in his left hand he held a scepter.

It was a day when all the heathen temples were open and decorated elaborately with sweet-smelling flowers. Incense was lit on every altar so that the victor was greeted with a cloud of perfume.[5]

Paul uses this analogy in writing about the believer being victorious in Christ Jesus. In 2 Corinthians 2:14,15, Paul thanks God who ALWAYS leads us in triumph. Christ Himself is the conqueror; we are trophies of His victory. Our prayers and our lives diffuse a sweet odor of Him wherever we go.

The following verses also refer to this analogy:

When He [God] had disarmed the rulers and authorities, He made a public display of them, having triumphed over them through Him [Christ] (Col. 2:15).

And when He had taken the book, the four living creatures and the twenty-four elders fell down before the Lamb, having each one a harp, and golden bowls full of incense, which are the prayers of the saints (Rev. 5:8).

Intercession is an incense before God's altar, and the prayers of the righteous do accomplish much (see Jas. 5:16). It is through intercession that the battle is won over the forces of darkness. You must constantly wear the armor of God to be able to withstand and overcome during this war.

On that day when the seal is broken in heaven and the trumpet sounds, may your prayers return unto Him as sweet-smelling incense before His throne. And may you be a fragrance of Christ unto God among those being saved and among those who are perishing.

On the next few pages you will find charts for each piece of the Armor of God, beginning with "Standing Firm" and ending with "The Whole Armor of God." The section will expand the meaning of each piece of armor based on Ephesians 6:14-17. The charts will contain an "Area of Protection," including the "Definition" and "Application," the "Affirmation" (Scriptures) and the "Declaration" for that piece of armor. When the enemy attacks, refer to the page where the appropriate piece of armor is listed. Read the Scriptures given and repeat the declaration.

Notes

1. Robert Young, *Young's Analytical Concordance to the Bible*, 22nd American Edition (Grand Rapids: William B. Eerdmans Publishing Company, 1955, reprinted 1983), pp. 299-300.
2. Ibid., p. 836.
3. C. S. Lewis, *Screwtape Letters* (New York: Macmillan Publishing, 1982).
4. William Gurnall, *The Christian in Complete Armour* (Lindale, Tex.: Banner of Truth Trust, 1991), pp. 140-141.
5. James M. Freeman, *Manners and Customs of the Bible* (South Plainfield, N.J.: Bridge Publishing, 1972), pp. 460-461.

Standing Firm
Area of Protection

Definition
To STAND means to resist without yielding; to maintain a position; to persist; to endure; to remain upright; to encounter; to meet face-to-face.

Application
As an heir and child of God, you are to STAND in that place that is already yours. It has been delivered to you through the cross of Jesus Christ.

Do not in any way surrender to an uprising of the enemy. Submit yourself to God; then STAND and resist the devil and he will flee.

Note: Jesus did not use the Word of God to attack the devil; He used it to maintain the victory He already had.

Declaration
Having done all, I am going to stand firm. I will not yield to the devil's schemes, but will hold fast to the Word of God.

I will stand in faith on the solid rock, Jesus. You are my foundation; I will not be moved by the roar of the enemy, nor by negative circumstances. I will stand valiant and strong, for with You on my side, who can be against me?

As a priest before You, O Lord, I will bless Your holy name and serve You in obedience.

I will stand in the victory that has been won, for the battle is not mine but Yours. In this way, I am more than a conqueror in Christ Jesus.

Affirmation
2 Chronicles 20:15,17

Joshua 1:9

1 Corinthians 16:13

Ephesians 6:11-14

Philippians 4:1

1 Thessalonians 3:6-8

2 Thessalonians 2:1-5

The Girdle or Belt of Truth
Area of Protection

Definition

LOINS are a picture of strength, power, vigor and maturity. They include the reproductive organs, the digestive system and the bowels. Weak loins disable a soldier. The GIRDLE or BELT, worn about the loins to brace him for the fight, was a symbol of a soldier's strength and superior ability. It kept the armor in place, and supported the sword; money and valuables were also carried here. To GIRD means to prepare oneself for action.

Application

A person whose mind is girded with truth will be strong and vigorous with mature spiritual insight, and will reproduce the Word of God for His glory. One who is double-minded is unstable in all his/her ways. TRUTH is the teaching presented in God's Word, embodied in Jesus Christ, revealed to us by the Holy Spirit. WE GIRD OURSELVES WITH TRUTH when we embrace and uphold God's revelation to us, and walk in agreement with Him.

Declaration

Jesus, You are my truth. You have made me to know the truth in my inward parts. I am dressed in readiness because Your truth clothes me.

I encompass my mind with Your truth so I am ready for action. I resist all double-mindedness, and claim that I have the mind of Christ.

I shall know the truth and the truth will set me free. I will speak forth the truth in love today. I will accurately handle the Word of truth, and will plant seeds of truth in others so You may be reproduced in them.

Thank You, Jesus, for choosing me from the foundation of the world for salvation through sanctification by the Spirit and faith in the truth.

Affirmation

Exodus 12:11

Deuteronomy 33:11

Psalm 51:6

Luke 12:35

John 8:32; 14:6

1 Corinthians 2:16

Ephesians 4:15; 6:14

2 Thessalonians 2:13

2 Timothy 2:15

James 1:8; 4:8

1 Peter 1:13

The Breastplate of Righteousness
Area of Protection

Definition
The BREASTPLATE, covering the soldier's vital organs (heart, lungs, liver, etc.), came down over the girdle or belt, increasing the protection of the loins. By protecting these vital organs, the breastplate emboldened a soldier to face the enemy without fear.

Application
RIGHTEOUSNESS—right-standing or uprightness before God—is imparted by Christ to the believer. This BREASTPLATE OF RIGHTEOUSNESS preserves the Christian's soul and conscience—the "vital organs" of the spirit-man. Thus the Christian is filled with courage, knowing he/she is protected by the righteousness of Christ and can face the enemy without fear.

Declaration
Jesus, You are my righteousness. In You I live and move and have my being. Help me to conform to Your character and Your will in my life.

I put on Your righteousness by faith and ask that You protect my heart, that I may walk with pure motives.

Help me to do that which is right and just, so that I might have a clear conscience and not be afraid of evil consequences. Thank You for courage to face the enemy without fear.

Thank You for cleansing me from my sins and restoring me to fellowship with You because You were the perfect sacrifice for my sins.

Affirmation
Proverbs 28:1

Isaiah 59:16-17

Romans 3:22,25,26

Romans 5:17-19

2 Corinthians 5:21

Ephesians 6:14

1 Thessalonians 5:8

1 John 1:7,9

The Shoes of the Gospel of Peace
Area of Protection

Definition
The phrase "preparation of the gospel of peace" means "to be ready, or dressed in readiness," which was vital when a soldier had to dodge, stand or run in hand-to-hand combat with the enemy. His SHOES had metal cleats, which made him more surefooted in battle.

Application
FEET represent your walk with the Lord. Your "walk" is the witness of your speech, your behavior and your attitude. SHOD means to bind under or to tie up; i.e., to be ready to receive marching orders. Shoes were removed upon entering a house, and put on again when going out. GOSPEL is the good news that Jesus Christ was crucified for our sins, was raised from the dead, and has defeated the enemy. PEACE is freedom from strife—inner peace which comes from God when conflict with the enemy rages without. It is a walk founded in reconciliation.

Declaration
Jesus, You are my peace. You have brought to my life wholeness and harmony with the Father. May Your peace sanctify me wholly—body, soul and spirit.

I shod my feet with Your gospel, Your peace. I desire to walk today in a quiet, unquarrelsome manner. Thank You for keeping my feet from harm, and guiding my path.

My feet will not be moved from the gospel, for I am not ashamed of the good news. Your gospel is the power of God for salvation to everyone who believes.

Because my feet are set securely in Your peace, I am ready to maneuver in any direction the Holy Spirit leads me. Keep me in a state of readiness so I can boldly tread upon enemy territory to set the captives free from Satan's bondage.

Affirmation
Exodus 12:11

1 Samuel 2:9

Psalm 18:33

Psalm 66:8,9

Isaiah 26:3

Matthew 12:18-21

Ephesians 6:15

Colossians 1:20

1 Thessalonians 5:23

The Shield of Faith
Area of Protection

Definition
The SHIELD, a defensive weapon, was usually carried on the left arm and was used to protect the entire body of a soldier. The surface was kept bright with oil, which reflected the sun to blind the enemy. It helped deflect the enemy's blows.

Application
A SHIELD represents protection and security; our shield of faith works in cooperation with the other pieces of armor to quench the fiery darts of doubt, fear and unbelief, and to blind the enemy. The mind and the will control its movements.

FAITH is simply believing, accepting and appropriating what God has said. FAITH requires a total trust in the Lord Jesus in all things.

Declaration
Lord Jesus, You are my shield of faith. My self nature has been crucified with You, and the life I now live, I live by faith in You. I will resist the devil by being firm in that faith.

Thank You for being a shield unto me. I put my trust in You, choosing to walk by faith, not by sight or circumstances. I will speak words of faith and I will ask in faith without doubting.

Your Word is Your power. Thank You, Father, that You are alert and active, watching over Your Word to perform it. It protects me from the evil one because..."It is written." The devil runs in terror from me because I draw near unto You and resist him in Jesus' name by lifting up this shield of faith which is anointed with the oil of Your Holy Spirit.

Affirmation
Proverbs 30:5

Jeremiah 1:12

2 Corinthians 5:7

Galatians 2:20

Ephesians 6:16

Colossians 1:10,11

Hebrews 10:22; 11:1

James 1:6; 4:7

1 Peter 1:5; 5:9

1 John 5:10

The Helmet of Salvation
Area of Protection

Definition

The HELMET was the armor worn by a soldier to protect his head. It often bore insignia or ornaments identifying the army to which the soldier belonged.

Application

The HELMET, the hope of salvation, guards your mind from the enemy's darts. Your mind directs the use of your shield and your sword and all movements of the body; thus it must be protected so you can be an effective soldier.

Your mind is the battleground between the flesh and the spirit; a disciplined soldier will not yield to the flesh, but will be strong in spirit.

Declaration

Jesus, You are my salvation. You have covered my head in the day of battle; You are my strength and song, and You have become my salvation.

I put my hope and trust in You. The helmet of hope shall be as a helmet of deliverance to me. You have set my mind free from the darts of the enemy.

Today I will renew my mind by the Word of God; I refuse to entertain the thoughts of doubt and unbelief the enemy would bring to me. I bring every thought into captivity to the obedience of Christ. I will concentrate on those things which pertain to life and peace. All praise be unto You, the God of my salvation!

Affirmation

Psalm 140:7

Isaiah 51:6; 59:16,17

Romans 8:6; 12:2

2 Corinthians 2:16; 10:5

Ephesians 4:23; 6:17

Colossians 3:2

1 Thessalonians 5:8

Titus 1:2; 3:7

Hebrews 5:9

1 Peter 1:13

YOU'RE IN A BATTLE 119

The Sword of the Spirit
Area of Protection

Definition
The SWORD was both defensive and offensive. It defended the soldier from the enemy's assault, and was used to wound or kill the enemy. It was wielded with the right arm, and was a symbol of power and authority.

Application
The SWORD OF THE SPIRIT is the Word of God quickened and made alive by the Holy Spirit; the wielding of this sword is only effective when the other pieces of armor are in place.

The WORD comes from your mouth. The Word of God is your power and authority when quickened by the Holy Spirit. It will judge the thoughts and intents of your own heart, and of the heart of the one spoken to.

Declaration
Lord Jesus, You are the Living Word. I go forth with praises in my mouth and a two-edged sword in my hand. Today I will confess Your Word before men, and You will confess me before the Father in heaven. Your words are true. Your Word is the foundation of the world. You are the joy and rejoicing of my heart because I have been called by Your name, and therefore have the authority to use this weapon. I will to speak forth Your Word in power. Your Word abides in me and I in You.

Your Word is quick and powerful and sharper than any two-edged sword; it divides between that which is spiritual or godly, and that which is soulish or of the flesh. Your Word is Your wisdom. The Holy Spirit will give me in the hour of need a mouth of wisdom which none of my opponents will be able to resist or refute.

Thank You, Lord Jesus, for giving me the provision of Your Word, my SWORD!

Affirmation
1 Samuel 17:51,54

Psalm 149:6

Jeremiah 15:16

Luke 21:15

John 1:1,14

1 Corinthians 1:30

Ephesians 6:17

Hebrews 1:3; 4:12

The Whole Armor of God

When the enemy attacks in these areas, refer to the page where the appropriate piece of armor is listed. Then read the Scriptures given and repeat the "Declaration."

Type of Attack

Lies against the character of God
Deception about who I am
Error as to the way I am going

Believing accusations from Satan
Feeling condemned
Puffed up with spiritual pride

Attacked by persecution or lies
Compromising the Word of God
Passive and asleep
Hit by a flaming missile of doubt,
    fear, or unbelief

Protection

Girdle of Truth
Breastplate of Righteousness
Shoes of the Gospel of Peace
Shield of Faith

Type of Attack

Having trouble with thoughts of guilt,
    condemnation, hatred toward others
Operating in the flesh and not the spirit
Remaining in darkness; unrenewed mind

Whispered words such as "Hath God said?"
Distortion of the Word of God
Word taken out of heart of the hearer
Listening to doctrines of demons

Protection

Helmet of Salvation
Sword of the Spirit

Section IV

Weapons
of Warfare

❦

8

The Christian Arsenal
Part 1

For though we walk in the flesh, we do not war
according to the flesh, for the weapons of our
warfare are not of the flesh, but divinely powerful
for the destruction of fortresses. We are destroying
speculations and every lofty thing raised up against
the knowledge of God, and we are taking every
thought captive to the obedience of Christ, and
we are ready to punish all disobedience,
whenever your obedience is complete.

—*2 Corinthians 10:3-6*

Every plan of God is for the good of His people; every plan of
Satan is for their destruction. Satan knows that when he wounds
one of God's people, he wounds the heart of God. The real war
is between God and Satan. We are not drafted, but we can enlist
in God's service. Then as soldiers in God's army, our commission
is to liberate those who are behind the enemy's lines by breaking his strongholds with the weapons of our warfare.

Satan's goal is to see that the prayers of God's people do not reach heaven because God has chosen to partner with His people in fulfilling His plans on earth. So when you come to God on behalf of others, often you will need to battle against the powers of darkness. Satan knows where people are weak and attempts to enter through that opening in their lives to take them captive. Any area where people are in bondage is an area where Satan has a strong hold or "stronghold" in their lives.

It is God's will for us to tear down those strongholds and loose people in areas where they have not been able to freely function. This is a primary purpose of the spiritual weapons God provides for us. As we war on earth, it stirs divine intervention from heaven.

The following diagram helps to illumine the complete arsenal of spiritual weapons every believer has at his or her disposal. The pillars that support this arsenal are *faith* and *obedience*, and *prayer* and *intercession*; these are essential for the effective implementation of the seven primary weapons. God has provided all that is necessary for successful spiritual warfare; your part is to will to use the weapons that His Word guarantees will destroy enemy strongholds.

"In warfare there are four possible attitudes—offense, defense, détente and desertion...Satan can get along very well with Christians as long as they are on the defensive, seeking détente or desert-

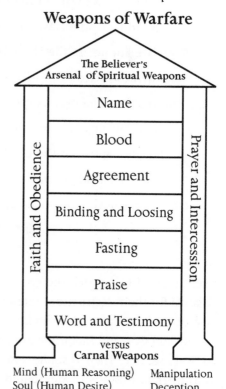

Weapons of Warfare

The Believer's
Arsenal of Spiritual Weapons

Name

Blood

Agreement

Binding and Loosing

Fasting

Praise

Word and Testimony

Faith and Obedience

Prayer and Intercession

versus
Carnal Weapons

Mind (Human Reasoning)   Manipulation
Soul (Human Desire)   Deception
Will   Control

THE CHRISTIAN ARSENAL—PART 1 127

ing. Therefore, if we are determined to see him defeated in our own hearts and in our society, we must be only and always committed to the offensive."[1]

Faith and Obedience: Our Pillar of Victory

Faith and *obedience* are so intertwined that one is incomplete without the other. These two factors go together to comprise one of the pillars that supports the believer's arsenal of spiritual weapons.

You must have *faith* that the weapons God provides for you will work and accomplish the desired purpose for His glory. Have *faith* in the name of Jesus. Have *faith* in the power of Jesus. Have *faith* that the same power dwells in you and empowers you to do even greater works than He did, because Jesus lives in you (see John 14:12). Listen to Jesus' words about faith:

> "Have faith in God. Truly I say to you, whoever says to this mountain 'Be taken up and cast into the sea,' and does not doubt in his heart, but believes that what he says is going to happen, it shall be granted him. Therefore I say to you, all things for which you pray and ask, believe that you have received them, and they shall be granted you" (Mark 11:22-24).

Exercise your faith by speaking forth the Word and declaring aloud the victory Christ gives. When the Holy Spirit quickens a verse of Scripture for a given situation, speak it forth as a word of faith, casting down every imagination that is contrary to the Word of God (see 2 Cor. 10:5).

What quenches all fear, doubt and unbelief? FAITH, FAITH, FAITH. BELIEVING, BELIEVING, BELIEVING.

You can speak forth faith as a command. Note the example in Acts 16:18: "But Paul was greatly annoyed, and turned and said to the spirit, 'I command you in the name of Jesus Christ to come out of her!' And it came out at that very moment."

The importance of *obedience*—which also includes commitment—cannot be overemphasized. As an intercessor, your work is going to be constant and challenging. You will be putting yourself in the place of the person for whom you are praying, sometimes feeling his or her need. This type of prayer calls for *obedience* to the voice of the Spirit and unwavering commitment. But a word of warning: *Do not allow intercession to keep you burdened.* Learn how to respond in obedience when the Spirit calls you to prayer, but then release prayer burdens to your loving heavenly Father.

Commitment means the act of entrusting to: delivered in trust. Therefore, your commitment and determination to withstand the enemy and aggressively oppose him will strengthen your warfare. The enemy recognizes this quality in you. Someone has aptly said that all hell trembles to see a saint on his knees. For this very reason, the enemy will try to keep you from prayer. Your *obedience* and commitment will foil his plan!

As a Christian you are set apart and consecrated to God for His sacred purpose. As you entrust your *life* to Him more and more every day, the world will notice a difference:

> And they overcame him because of the blood of the Lamb and because of the word of their testimony, *and they did not love their life even to death* (Rev. 12:11, italics added).

Your *life* is now "hidden with Christ in God" (Col. 3:3). Since He laid down His *life* for you, you should lay down your *life* for the brethren (see 1 John 3:16).

"It is a trustworthy statement: For if we died with Him, we shall also live with Him; if we endure, we shall also reign with Him; if we deny Him, He also will deny us; if we are faithless, He remains faithful; for He cannot deny Himself" (2 Tim. 2:11-13).

Prayer and Intercession: The Pillar of Communication and Power

We have already discussed in previous chapters the importance of communication with God and the difference between prayer and intercession. *Prayer* and *intercession* comprise the other pillar that supports the arsenal of spiritual weapons.

Here we will discuss the matter of praying in the Spirit. The term "praying in the Spirit" can mean different things to different people or denominations.

To some it means following the leading of the Holy Spirit and praying as He directs in your understanding or in song. As you pray earnestly, you follow the prompting of the Spirit deep within your spirit. These prayers may be prayed from the heart or from written prayers, using books such as *My Utmost for His Highest* by Oswald Chambers, *Prayers That Avail Much* by Word Ministries, Inc., or the prayers in the section of this book titled "Daily Prayers," chapter 10.

To others praying in the Spirit may mean praying in an unknown tongue as described in 1 Corinthians 14:1-25. Private "praying in tongues" is different than the use of tongues and interpretation of tongues in public worship (see 1 Cor. 14:26-28). As you read the following Scriptures, you will notice that this form of praying in the Spirit can be a useful tool for some intercessors.

1. **Praying in the Spirit is your spirit communicating directly with God.** It is primarily for use in your devotional prayer life for intercession, praise and worship:

Let him speak to himself and to God (1 Cor. 14:28b).

For one who speaks in a tongue does not speak to men, but to God; for no one understands, but in his spirit he speaks mysteries (1 Cor. 14:2).

2. **Praying in the Spirit is a perfect prayer.** Since you do not always know how or what to pray in a given situation, you can bring the need before the Lord by praying in the Spirit. The Holy Spirit, your Helper, enables you to pray as you ought—thereby praying in the Lord's will.

Praying in the Spirit is a means by which the Holy Spirit intercedes through your spirit in prayer. This is where we get the term "prayer language," an unlearned language in which you can pray. When you pray with your understanding, you are easily influenced by your feelings, thoughts, desires, experiences, distractions, understanding and will. Even your vocabulary can limit your prayers. God gives you a prayer language that bypasses your mind, will and emotions and allows you to continue in prayer without interruption:

> And in the same way the Spirit also helps our weakness; for we do not know how to pray as we should, but the Spirit Himself intercedes for us with groanings too deep for words; and He who searches the hearts knows what the mind of the Spirit is, because He intercedes for the saints according to the will of God. And we know that God causes all things to work together for good to those who love God, to those who are called according to His purpose (Rom. 8:26-28).

> (See also 1 Cor. 14:14; 1 John 5:14,15; Jas. 4:3).

3. Praying in the Spirit has definite meaning. Although you do not understand what you are praying, God does:

> There are, perhaps, a great many kinds of languages in the world, and no kind is without meaning (1 Cor. 14:10).

4. Praying in the Spirit edifies the person praying. When you are built up, strengthened and encouraged, you can continue with the spiritual warfare you are called to do:

> One who speaks in a tongue edifies himself (1 Cor. 14:4a).

> But you, beloved, building yourselves up on your most holy faith; praying in the Holy Spirit (Jude 20).

5. Praying in the Spirit has the authority of heaven behind it. There is no way you could know when Satan and his demonic forces will launch an attack. The Holy Spirit will prompt you at the strategic, opportune time:

> With all prayer and petition pray at all times in the Spirit, and with this in view, be on the alert with all perseverance and petition for all the saints (Eph. 6:18).
>
> (See also Eph. 6:12; Jas. 5:16b).

Praying is an act of your will, whether you are praying in the Spirit or with your understanding. When Peter walked on the water, he had to exercise his will and faith. He got out of the boat and moved his feet. Walking was not the miracle; the fact that he didn't sink was.

Praying in the Spirit is similar. You must respond to the Holy Spirit's prompting in the same way—with faith and obedience. Speaking is not the miracle; the fact that you speak in a language you don't understand is. The Holy Spirit will give you the utterance. As with any language, the more you use it, the more comfortable you will feel using it.

If you pray in tongues, it is important that you do not criticize, condemn or exclude those who don't. On the other hand, it is just as important to remember that if you do not pray in tongues, you refrain from the same attitudes or judgments of those who do. The issue is not how you pray, but that you are faithful to the call of prayer and led by the Spirit.

The apostle Paul wrote, "Now I wish that you all spoke in tongues....I thank God, I speak in tongues more than you all....Do not forbid to speak in tongues" (1 Cor. 14:5,18,39).

Communication with the Lord through prayer and intercession is a pillar on which our life in Christ depends. It is a strong pillar of support in the Christian's arsenal of spiritual weapons against the enemy. Praying and singing in the Spirit is the power that moves mountains and draws you into fellowship with the Lord:

> What is the outcome then? I shall pray with the spirit and I shall pray with the mind also; I shall sing with the spirit and I shall sing with the mind also (1 Cor. 14:15).

The Name of Jesus: Our Authority

As you pray in the Spirit, you will need to take your authority in Christ. The name of *Jesus* has power on earth, and in heaven and hell. Since you are a temple of His Spirit and the same Holy Spirit dwells in you, you can use His name just as though He Himself were here. "I have given you authority...over all the power of the enemy" (Luke 10:19), Jesus promised.

Jesus gave His followers power and authority over demons, and He gave them the right to ask the Father for things *in His name*:

> And whatever you ask in My name, that will I do, that the Father may be glorified in the Son. If you ask Me anything in My name, I will do it (John 14:13,14).

> Therefore also God highly exalted Him, and bestowed on Him the name which is above every name, that at the name of Jesus every knee should bow, of those who are in heaven, and on earth, and under the earth (Phil. 2:9,10).

Everything has to bow at the name of Jesus. So use the name of JESUS during warfare. God recognizes it. And so does the devil and his host of fallen angels. Make the enemy flee in terror. Say the name of our Lord Jesus.

The following is an effective way to pray using Jesus' name and authority:

> By the authority of Jesus and His precious blood, I bind you, Satan, according to Ephesians 6:12 and break your powers over this situation. I loose (name of person) from your hold and destroy your works and your assignment in Jesus' name.

> Father, I ask that Your will now be done, and I thank you. In Jesus' name and by His authority, I declare it done.

The power of the Holy Spirit in you gives you authority to use the name of Jesus to defeat the enemy. It can be likened to a policeman who can halt a huge truck just by standing in the middle of the highway and holding up his hand to signal "Stop!" The policeman, wearing his badge, has authority behind him to stop traffic and forbid the truck to proceed when a law has been violated. Intercessors, too, must use their delegated authority to stop demonic forces from wreaking havoc with God's people.

> But the one who joins himself to the Lord is one spirit with Him (1 Cor. 6:17).

> (See also Eph. 3:16; Rom. 8:11.)

A key to your authority in using the name of Jesus is your personal relationship with Him. That relationship, nurtured by your time of fellowship with the Lord, ensures that you will use this authority *only* in ways that will glorify Him. Notice the example of Peter and John speaking to the lame man at the temple gate in Acts 3:1-8. On the other hand, note what happened to those who tried to use the name of Jesus without proper authority in Acts 19:11-17. If you are walking in proper relationship to Jesus Christ, the enemy must submit to your authority when you use the name of Jesus:

> And these signs will accompany those who have believed: in My name they will cast out demons, they will speak with new tongues; they will pick up serpents, and if they drink any deadly poison, it shall not hurt them; they will lay hands on the sick, and they will recover (Mark 16:17,18).

The name of Jesus is your power of attorney and the blood of Jesus is the official seal that secures your right to use it.

The Blood of Jesus: Our Covering

When God released the plague of death against Egypt, forcing Pharaoh to free the Jews, God instructed the Jewish people to put the blood of an unblemished lamb over the doorposts of their homes. The angel of death then passed over every house that was covered with the blood of the lamb. (Read Exodus 12.) Today Jesus, the perfect Lamb of God, offers the same kind of protection through the power of His innocent blood shed on Calvary for all those who believe.

I can personally testify to times when the blood of Jesus has protected me from an onslaught of the enemy. For example, in February of 1976 Floyd and I purchased a van to give to a church in Guatemala. When we arrived there, we met with the pastor to discuss the details of the seminar we would be teaching. Then he gave us directions for getting to the beautiful little guest house which had been prepared for us just outside of town. As we were walking out the door, the pastor said that if we did not want to stay at the guest house, we could use the apartment directly above the church. He gave us the key, so we thanked him and went on our way.

Our van was packed with supplies to give to the Guatemalan pastors. Therefore, every time we reached another checkpoint, we had to open up the van and allow the officials to search through all our things. By the time we arrived at the guest house, we were exhausted. Because we had to be back in town by 8 A.M. the following morning, we realized that with the delays at the checkpoints, we would probably not make it. So we returned to the church late that same night and dragged our tired bodies into the church apartment.

It was now 2 A.M. and I was just laying my head on the pillow when the Lord began to speak to me about changing my message for the following day. I slipped out of bed and waited for my orders. He directed me to Isaiah 41, where I read:

The coastlands have seen and are afraid; the ends of the earth tremble; they have drawn near and have come. Each one helps his neighbor, and says to his brother, "Be strong!"

"But you, Israel, My servant, Jacob whom I have chosen, descendant of Abraham My friend, you whom I have taken from the ends of the earth, and called from its remotest parts, and said to you, 'You are My servant, I have chosen you and not rejected you. Do not fear, for I am with you; do not anxiously look about you, for I am your God. I will strengthen you, surely I will help you, surely I will uphold you with My righteous right hand'" (vv. 5,6,8-10).

I knew this was to be my text for the following day, but I was not quite sure what the message would be when I crawled back into bed at 3 A.M. I had just found a half-suitable position upon the mattress when I began to hear animals howling outside. At first I thought the sounds might be demonic. Then I heard the pitter patter of dogs running across the flat roof above me. Suddenly the entire building began to shake with such force that I was nearly thrust out of bed. All I could think of were my daughters who were sleeping in the next room. I put both feet on the floor and was hurled across the room with such might that my watch broke as I slammed into the wall. I heard one of the girls say, "Is this the rapture?"

The other responded, "No, cause we're not going up!"

Little did I know that many of the prophetic voices in this town had warned the people of God's coming judgment for the sins of drunkenness, adultery, witchcraft and idolatry. The morning after the earthquake hit, there were 60 couples standing outside the church repenting before God and asking to be married. (*National Geographic* magazine reported 23,000 people killed in one day, resembling the report in 1 Corinthians 10:1-8.)

When we returned to see the little guest house where we had intended to stay, the hairs on my arms stood on end. The house had crumbled and a huge cement beam lay stretched across the beds where Floyd and I and our two daughters would have slept. Immediately I could see in the theater of my mind an instant replay of the prayer our pastor had prayed for us before we left on our trip. He had laid his hands on each member of our family, asking for God's protection and began to plead the blood of Jesus over us. Thank God for the blood of Jesus that washes away our sins and causes the wicked plans of the enemy to pass over us. (See Heb. 9:12-14.)

"Pleading the blood of Jesus" is a tactic for intercession that has been used by prayer warriors for many, many years. Because of abuse, however, it has become somewhat controversial. To "plead the blood of Jesus" over a person for his or her protection is simply to remind the enemy of his boundaries. (See Exod. 12:22,23.)

The blood of Jesus secures lasting peace and victory. A fore-shadowing of this is seen in 1 Samuel 7:3-14 when Samuel challenged Israel to destroy the false gods of the Philistines which had polluted the land. The people responded in obedience and observed a day of fasting. The Philistines were angered when they heard their idols had been destroyed, so they staged an attack. The people said to Samuel, "Do not cease to cry to the Lord our God for us, that He may save us from the hand of the Philistines" (v. 8). Samuel responded by taking a suckling lamb and offering it as a whole offering to the Lord.

In his book, *Born for Battle*, Arthur Matthews sums up the account:

> Standing identified with the complete acceptance of his lamb, Samuel cries unto the Lord for Israel. The Lord thunders from heaven, the Philistines are frightened off, and, according to the record, "came no more into the coast of Israel."

> The victory was necessary to the peace. Peace is victory sustained. The only man who can keep the enemy at bay is the intercessor, and blessed is that intercessor who knows how to use the power of the blood in spiritual warfare.
> "Precious blood, by this we conquer
> In the fiercest fight,
> Sin and Satan overcoming
> by its might."
> —F. R. Havergal[2]

Blood-Bought Benefits
The blood of Jesus:

- Gives SALVATION. Births us into His kingdom and keeps us from eternal damnation (see Mark 16:16; John 3:3,17).

- Makes ATONEMENT for us, blotting out sins (see Lev. 17:11; Rom. 5:11).
- REDEEMS us. Our life is paid for in full, bought back from the power of sin and death (see Ps. 107:2; Eph. 1:7; Heb. 9:12; Rev. 5:9).
- JUSTIFIES us. Acquits us of sin and guilt (see Acts 13:38,39; Rom. 5:9).
- Makes us RIGHTEOUS. Puts us back into right standing with God (see Isa. 59:2; Rom. 3:22,23,25; 1 John 1:9).
- Gives SANCTIFICATION. Sets us apart unto God at the time of salvation as well as each day thereafter through the blood of Jesus (see 1 Cor. 1:30; Heb. 10:10,14).
- Allows REMISSION of sins. Sin was canceled (see Rom. 3:24,25; Heb. 9:22).
- RECONCILES us. Accepting God's provision, we can now fellowship with Him in love (see Rom. 5:10; Col. 1:20).
- Gives OVERCOMING POWER as we receive and use what has been delegated to us (see Luke 10:19; Rev. 12:11).
- Provides DELIVERANCE. Releases us from powers of darkness and sets us free (see 2 Cor. 2:14; Col. 1:13).
- Releases FORGIVENESS. Pardons sins (see Col. 1:14; 1 John 1:9).
- Establishes a NEW COVENANT. Replaces old covenant of sacrifices; perfect sacrifice now has been made through Jesus Christ (see Heb. 7:22; 8:13; 9:15; 10:9; 12:24).
- CLEANSES us from all sin (see 1 John 1:7).

Agreement: Our Bonding

Intercessors *agree* with the Holy Spirit on that which He has called them to accomplish through spiritual warfare. "Agreement" means "to harmonize, to live in concord, without contention." We are all called to be consistent with our prayers by the Word and by the Spirit. And to be consistent, we must keep our hearts free from division so we remain unified within the Body of believers.

Agreement, or unity, can be both an offensive and a defensive weapon. When a wolf wants to kill a lamb, he waits until it strays from the flock. The lamb is then unable to defend itself because it is alone. And yet, within the company of others, it is protected. We find safety by bonding in agreement with other believers and staying close to the Shepherd.

Agreement begins with a God focus and a heart that is close to Him. When your heart is knit to the Lord, He then will knit you together with another to accomplish more than you could ever accomplish alone. This is the "threefold cord" that Solomon wrote about in Ecclesiastes 4:12. "Two are better than one because they have a good return for their labor. For if either of them falls, the one will lift up his companion. But woe to the one who falls when there is not another to lift him up. And if one can overpower him who is alone, two can resist him" (vv. 9,10,12).

Before you can pray in agreement, you must learn to be in one accord with another intercessor (see Acts 2:1). Partnerships strengthen and protect your position in the army of God. Prayer alliances with others of like spirit can increase your warfare efforts. However, choose prayer partners very carefully under the direction of the Holy Spirit; human logic must not be the determining factor in such a choice.

When your heart is knit to the Lord, He then will
knit you together with another to accomplish more
than you could ever accomplish alone.

If it is just one partner, the person should be of your same sex, and should be accessible for frequent communication. If you feel the Lord is leading you toward a specific individual as a prayer partner, and the feeling is mutual, test the relationship. Is the relationship pure, holy and above reproach? Are there any hidden motives? Would the Lord be pleased?

Jesus said:

"Again I say to you, that if two of you agree on earth about anything that they may ask, it shall be done for them by My Father who is in heaven. For where two or three have gathered together in My name, there I am in their midst" (Matt. 18:19,20).

Learning to pray in agreement is learning to pray in God's will. As your mind is transformed, you will discover the perfect will of God and be in agreement with Him through His Word. (See Rom. 12:2.)

There is a warning about what could happen if you are in agreement over something ungodly. Read Acts 5:1,2 and 9, and you will see that when Ananias and his wife Sapphira agreed to tell a lie, their plot cost them their lives. "Why is it that you have agreed together to put the Spirit of the Lord to the test?" Peter asked Sapphira just before she fell over dead.

You may ask, "What if I make a mistake?" If your heart is right and your motives pure, God's grace will abound.

Learn to discern the spirit of the one with whom you are agreeing. If you agree with the word of the enemy—by listening to bad reports he whispers in your ear or sends by way of someone else—you are in wrong agreement. Agree with what the Word tells you or the Holy Spirit brings to your mind.

Invite the Holy Spirit to be present before you even start to pray. Pray in one accord with Him.

Binding and Loosing: Our Keys

Once you have come into agreement with the Holy Spirit, you will need to use your power of attorney in Christ Jesus to stop the plans of hell and release the purposes of heaven. Jesus has given His followers two effective weapons for doing this: *binding* and *loosing*. They are Kingdom keys used to put a lock on Satan's power and unlock the power of God.

I will give you the keys of the kingdom of heaven; and whatever you shall bind on earth shall have been bound in heaven, and whatever you shall loose on earth shall have been loosed in heaven (Matt. 16:19).

What then is the meaning of the phrase, "shall be bound in heaven...shall be loosed in heaven"? One Bible translator points out that the verb form is the perfect passive participle, *so the reference is to things in a state of having been already forbidden (or permitted)*. This tells us that whatever is bound or loosed by the believer is done on the basis that it has already been done "in heaven."

"Or how can anyone enter the strong man's house and carry off his property, unless he first binds the strong man? And then he will plunder his house" (Matt. 12:29).

The context of this passage finds Jesus casting out demons. The Greek word for "bind" in the verse means "to fasten or tie—as with chains—as an animal tied to keep from leaving."[3]

Binding and loosing is not some kind of spiritual magic and cannot be used at every whim, such as, "Satan, I bind you off of my lottery ticket." This is an example of improper binding. It is contrary to the Word of God and would be for selfish purposes. It has nothing to do with binding and loosing for Kingdom purposes.

One author has this to say about binding and loosing: "It has to do with the authority of the Christian in spiritual warfare, and there are often many factors involved. Binding and loosing is a confident assurance and confession of God's order and government over against the disorder of a sin-cursed, demonized world."[4]

The Dictionary of New Testament Theology says, "The idea of binding may also refer back to the picture of the binding of the strong man (that is, Satan) who must first be bound before his goods (that is, those enthralled by him) may be plundered (see Matt. 12:29 Parallel; Mark 3:27; see also Luke 11:21). Thus Peter would be promised the power that Christ had to bind the powers of evil and to liberate men, and this would hold good not only on earth, but also in heaven."[5]

In order to bind the strong man, you must first know who the strong man is. It can be a principality, power, ruler of darkness in this world or a spiritual wickedness in high places (see Eph. 6:12). This is discerned through prayer and must always be within the will and timing of God. Many times fasting must accompany that prayer. When the man asked Jesus why His disciples could not cast the demon out of his son, He replied, "But this kind does not go out except by prayer and fasting." (See Matt. 17:14-21.)

Every individual believer has the right and authority to call down or resist the devil and bind the strong man. You as an individual will be singled out and challenged by the spirits of darkness. Or you will be called into war against the powers over your home, church, city, etc.

Binding and loosing demonic spirits or powers of higher-level spiritual dominion is definitely something you do not want to do without knowledge of what you are doing. When calling down strongholds, you may assist another in prayer and agreement as you learn, but never work alone. You must know your spiritual jurisdiction.

There can be serious repercussions if this is done outside of the realm of authority directly related to the order and authority of the Church. The hierarchy of darkness (see Eph. 6:12) understands authority and the chain of command of God's people. Moving without the proper authority is very dangerous to you and can create havoc within the church, etc., in which you are ministering.

To what then does the *loosing* refer? To setting the captive free! Do you recall the story of Jesus healing the woman who had a spirit of infirmity for 18 years? Jesus told her, "Woman, thou art loosed from thine infirmity." (See Luke 13:11,12, *KJV*.)

The Greek word for "loose" is defined in the lexicon as "to loose anything tied or fastened; to loose one bound; to set free; to discharge from prison. To free from bondage or disease (one held by Satan) by restoration to health."[6]

James M. Freeman, in his book *Manners and Customs of the Bible*, explains the common usage in Jewish schools for the words "bind" and "loose." To "bind" is to "forbid," and to "loose" is to "allow." Binding and loosing is prohibiting and permitting. In the Aramaic language, which Jesus used, it was a customary expression to denote the highest authority.

Jesus gave Peter the keys of the kingdom of heaven. When Jesus asked Peter who He was, Peter said, "Thou art the Christ, the Son of the living God" (Matt. 16:16). Then Jesus went on to say, "Upon this rock (revelation) will I build My church; and the gates of Hades shall not overpower it. I will give you the keys of the kingdom of heaven: and whatever you shall bind on earth shall be bound in heaven, and whatever you shall loose on earth shall be loosed in heaven" (vv. 18,19). Not only did Jesus give the keys to Peter, but He gave them to His Church as well.

To *bind* is to secure the enemy with pressure so he cannot move. To *loose* is to gain liberty using the Word of God. Binding refers to the enemy, while loosing refers to the victory.

There is no formula for binding and loosing. It must be done by revelation of His Spirit; however, the following is an example of the way you might pray in dealing with the devil concerning a loved one:

> I speak to you, Satan, in the mighty and precious name of Jesus Christ of Nazareth. I take authority over you and bind all demonic spirits assigned to (name of person). Loose (name of person) and let him go free in the name of Jesus. I demand that you stop your maneuvers against this child of God. (name of person) is covered by the blood of Jesus, the precious Lamb slain for him.

> (You might bind anything the Lord speaks to your heart as you pray. The Spirit of the Lord will lead you.)

> Lord, I ask that Your will now be done, and I thank You. In Jesus' name and by His authority, I declare it done.

Thank You, Lord, for watching over Your Word to perform it, in Jesus' name. Amen.

Now that you understand your Kingdom authority, you are ready to become a praying warrior. This will be accomplished as you learn to buffet your body and enter into the power available through a disciplined Christian life.

Notes

1. R. Arthur Matthews, *Born for Battle* (Robesonia, Pa.: OMF Books, 1978), p. 51.
2. Ibid., p. 63.
3. James Strong, *The New Strong's Exhaustive Concordance of the Bible* (New York: Thomas Nelson Publishers, 1984), #1210.
4. Gary Kinnaman, *Overcoming the Dominion of Darkness* (Grand Rapids: Chosen Books, 1990).
5. Colin Brown, ed., *The Dictionary of New Testament Theology, Vol. 2* (Grand Rapids: Zondervan, 1986), p. 733.
6. Walter Bauer, William F. Arndt, F. Wilbur Gingrich and Frederick W. Danker, *A Greek-English Lexicon of the New Testament and Other Early Christian Literature* (Chicago: University of Chicago Press, 1979; a reprint of the 1957 edition), p. 483. See also *Strong's* #3089.

9

The Christian Arsenal Part 2

All discipline for the moment seems not to be
joyful, but sorrowful; yet to those who have
been trained by it, afterwards it yields the
peaceful fruit of righteousness.

—*Hebrews 12:11*

When a soldier enlists in the military, the first eight weeks are
spent in boot camp, training the body for combat. The physical
body then becomes an extension of the soldier's arsenal. In much
the same way, when Christians discipline themselves through
prayer and fasting and reading the Word, their lives become part
of God's spiritual armory on earth in which His Body can be used
to demolish spiritual barriers and set the captives free.

Fasting: Our Cutting Edge

One of the most important disciplines for God's warriors to cul-
tivate is fasting. When you couple fasting with prayer, your
prayers transcend earthly understanding and bring about super-

natural breakthrough. Fasting is more than just abstaining from food; it is an act of self-denial for higher purposes. Therefore, it is important to check your motives and heart attitudes with the Lord before you determine to fast:

> "And whenever you fast, do not put on a gloomy face as the hypocrites do, for they neglect their appearance in order to be seen fasting by men. Truly I say to you, they have their reward in full. But you, when you fast, anoint your head, and wash your face so that you may not be seen fasting by men, but by your Father who is in secret; and your Father who sees in secret will repay you" (Matt. 6:16-18).

Notice that Jesus did not say "if" you fast, but "when" you fast. He expected Christians to use that discipline in their prayer lives. What is fasting? It is the voluntary and deliberate abstinence from food for the purpose of concentrated prayer. Jesus dealt with our motives for fasting and said we should never fast to impress others.

Being full of the Holy Spirit does not necessarily mean you walk in the *power* of the Spirit. One way into power is fasting and prayer (see Luke 4:1,2,14), which makes you much more spiritually sensitive to the Word of God and hearing His voice. This sensitivity to the Holy Spirit causes more power in your life to combat the forces of Satan.

When the Bridegroom is taken away, the disciples fast (see Matt. 9:14,15); it is a spiritual discipline (see 2 Cor. 6:5), which is shown in the New Testament as a means of gaining direction from the Holy Spirit, giving clarity of mind and spirit (see Acts 13:1-3; 14:21-23).

What is accomplished by fasting? Probably more than you will ever know until you get to heaven (see Isa. 58:6; Joel 1:14). I have seen incredible breakthroughs from my own fasting and heard wonderful testimonies from others who have fasted as well. In 1979 I was asked to speak to a group of people in western Kansas. I traveled through a blizzard to get there, so I was tired and drained when I arrived. I was escorted into the banquet room of a restaurant where nine people greeted me for dinner. Suddenly I heard the inner voice of the Holy Spirit speak into my mind, *I want you to give a word to each person here tonight.* I was fatigued from the trip, but I knew God could and would sustain me—after all, it was only nine people.

Suddenly the accordion wall behind us opened up and there sat an additional 79 men and women. I now realized it was going to be a very long evening. As I began to speak, the face of one woman kept distracting me. I kept seeing written across her forehead the words from a bumper sticker, "Keep on truckin'!" I thought, *Lord, am I seeing correctly?* I would give three or four more words and then look back at that woman. The words "Keep on truckin'!" continued to light up like a neon sign across her forehead. I had spoken to every person except this woman when I looked at her and said, "God would say to you, 'Keep on truckin!'" A thunderous shout erupted from the crowd and everyone began to applaud.

I then learned that the reason only nine people had attended the dinner was that the group had been fasting for this dear lady whose husband had recently died. Prior to his death, she and her husband used some of the profits from their trucking company to send two students through medical school each year. Now she and her friends were fasting and praying to know whether or not she should sell the company. The word for her that night confirmed that she was to keep it.

Surprisingly, I ran into this widow 10 years later and learned that she had supported many more students through med school and eventually sold the company for several times what it was worth when her husband died. Fasting not only brought life-changing revelation to this dear widow but also released the funds for God's will to be financed in the lives of others.

The following are some of the biblical reasons for fasting:

- Jesus set an example by spending 40 days fasting in the desert. (See Matt. 4:2; Luke 4:2.)
- As a freewill offering to the Father, it pleases Him. (See 1 Sam. 7:5,6; Acts 14:23.)

- It produces a spiritual and physical discipline. (See Luke 2:36,37; 1 Cor. 9:26,27.)
- It keeps you from God's judgments. (See Joel 2:12-14; John 3:5-10.)
- It manifests concern for family, church, community and country. (See 2 Sam. 1:12; 12:16; Ezra 8:21; Esther 4:3,16; Dan. 9:3; Matt. 9:15; Mark 2:18-20; Luke 5:33-35.)

Fasting has the following benefits:
- It strengthens and implements prayer. (See Acts 10:30,31.)
- It brings blessings of obedience. (See Matt. 6:6,16.)
- It brings humility through repentance. (See Neh. 9:1-3.)
- It gives revelation of God's way and will for your future. (See Dan. 9.)
- It establishes authority and power in prayer and spiritual warfare. (See Matt. 4:1-11.)

Fasting brings great victories. For example, King Jehoshophat called for a national fast against invading armies. As a result of the fast, the enemies killed each other (see 2 Chron. 20:1-30).

Fasting gives you a proper mental attitude: Don't view fasting as punishment, even though your body may rebel at first. Instead, view it as a precious opportunity to get closer to the Lord. When you fast, you are not distracted by the daily focus of eating. And the time that you would normally spend at the kitchen table can be set aside to feast from the spiritual food that God will serve you as you spend time in His presence at His table. God responds to your sincerity when you willingly humble yourself.

The following are some ways to fast:

- **Twenty-four-hour fast:** From sunset to sunset. Abstain from solids.
- **Partial fast:** Abstain from pleasant foods. Partake only of clear soups, fruit juices, cereals or grains, OR give up one meal a day for prayer. (See Dan. 1:8-16; 10:2,3.)
- **Three-day fast:** Total abstinence of food for three days. (See example in Esther 4:16.)

- **Extended fast:** Has two methods; both require preparation. Before an extended fast, it is recommended you omit caffeine and rich foods from your diet.
- **Total fast:** Excludes all food but does include water. Fast should be broken slowly. Only diluted juices for a day or two. Next gradually proceed to fruits, vegetables and grains, adding meats last.
- **Non-total fast:** No food intake; only diluted fruit juices, water and hot herbal teas are taken.

Note: *If you are on medication, consult your physician before commencing an extended fast.* You may need to consider a partial fast. Fast when directed by the Holy Spirit and according to your disciplined prayer life (see Isa. 58:6; 1 Cor. 9:26,27).

Use your fast as an opportunity to pray more. During this time your spirit is much more sensitive to the Holy Spirit, and you often will receive keener revelation from God's Word. Fasting is not an endurance test nor a religious ritual. It is a privilege and blessing to approach the Lord in humility and wholehearted faith.

Scriptures on fasting:

Exodus 34:28	Moses
Leviticus 16:29-31	Day of Atonement
Leviticus 23:27-32	Day of Atonement
1 Samuel 1:7,8	Hannah's prayer
2 Samuel 12:16-23	David for Bathsheba's child
1 Kings 13:8-24	Elijah
1 Kings 19:8	Elijah's journey to Horeb
1 Kings 21:27.	By Ahab in self-humiliation
2 Chronicles 20:3	Proclaimed by Jehoshaphat
Ezra 8:21-23	Proclaimed by Ezra
Nehemiah 1:4	By Nehemiah
Nehemiah 9:1	People of Jerusalem confessing sin
Esther 4:16	Called by Esther
Job 33:19,20	As a result of sickness and pain
Isaiah 58	Fasting which pleases God

Jeremiah 14:12 . . . . .That which is unacceptable
Joel 2:12 . . . . .Returning to God with whole heart
Matthew 6:16-18 . . . . .Not as hypocrites do
Matthew 17:21 . . . . .Only by prayer and fasting
Luke 2:37 . . . . .Anna worshiping in temple
Luke 4:2 . . . . .Jesus' 40-day fast
Luke 18:12 . . . . .Self-righteous and boastful
Acts 9:9 . . . . .Saul of Tarsus
Acts 10:30 . . . . .Cornelius when angel appeared
Acts 13:2,3 . . . . .By prophets and teachers in Antioch
Acts 14:23 . . . . .At appointment of elders
Romans 14:21 . . . . .Abstaining for sake of weaker one
1 Corinthians 7:5 . . . . . . .In marriage relationship
2 Corinthians 6:5 . . . . . . .Ingredient of Apostolic ministry
(from *God's Chosen Fast*, by Arthur Wallis)[1]

See fasting as a means for creating greater prayer focus. I like to equate the effects of fasting with laser surgery. The laser beam concentrates light to cut and correct physical problems. Likewise, fasting is a concentration of spiritual light on a problem to cut away the ideas of the flesh so God's answers can heal the situation. Fast with a definite goal to break the bondage and opposition of Satan. Fasting that glorifies God is birthed out of humility. It is more than just refraining from food; it is a mindset that says, "I can't; Jesus can."

Note: Before attempting a prolonged fast, become victorious with the shorter kinds of fasts, such as one-day or partial fasts.

Praise: Our Banner

Praise is another important discipline that is key to successful spiritual warfare. It is one of the most powerful weapons available to the believer. Jesus modeled *praise* by teaching His disciples to start and end their prayers with it. Don't wait to win the victories before you start *praising*; use it to lay the groundwork for the victories the Holy Spirit desires. You actually do battle from

THE CHRISTIAN ARSENAL—PART 2   151

a position of victory (see Eph. 1:20-22). Look at the example of Paul and Silas:

> And when they had inflicted many blows upon them, they threw them into prison, commanding the jailer to guard them securely; and he, having received such a command, threw them into the inner prison, and fastened their feet in the stocks. But about midnight Paul and Silas were praying and singing hymns of praise to God, and the prisoners were listening to them; and suddenly there came a great earthquake, so that the foundations of the prison house were shaken; and immediately all the doors were opened, and everyone's chains were unfastened (Acts 16:23-26).

(See also Rev. 19:5; Pss. 71:8; 150:6.)

What does praise do?
- It blesses the Lord (see Ps. 66:8; Luke 24:52,53).
- It brings you into His presence and draws you closer to Him (see Ps. 100:4).
- It opens doors and makes rough places smooth (see Isa. 60:18; Acts 16:25,26).
- It defeats the devil (see 2 Kings 11:13,14; Ps. 149:5-9).
- It brings revival (see 2 Chron. 31:2; 34:12; Ps. 107:32).
- It keeps you happy and gives you joy (see Isa. 61:1-3; Acts 2:45-47).

Praise is an act of body worship. When you worship God, you express a variety of emotions with your body. The following are examples of body worship through praise:

- When you clap your hands and stomp your feet, you portray your excitement (see 2 Kings 11:12; Ps. 98:8; Isa. 55:12; Lam. 2:15; Ezek. 6:11).
- When you stand up, march or walk, you portray readiness to serve or to go (see Gen. 13:17; Deut. 11:22-25; Josh. 1:1-5; Ps. 68:7,8).

- When you lift up your hands, you are worshiping and surrendering to God (see Exod. 17:8-16; 1 Kings 8:22-24; Pss. 28:2; 63:3,4; 134:2; 141:2; Luke 24:50,51; 1 Tim. 2:8; Heb. 12:12).
- When you dance, you express great joy (see 1 Sam. 18:6,7; Pss. 30:11; 149:3; Jer. 31:13; Luke 15:11-24).
- When you sing, you express gladness of heart (see Pss. 68:25; 100:2; 108:1; Prov. 29:6; Isa. 26:19; 65:13,14; Jer. 31:7; Zech. 2:10; 1 Cor. 14:15; Jas. 5:13; Rev. 15:3).
- When you play skillfully on an instrument, you show forth adoration (see 1 Sam. 16:23; 18:6,7; 1 Chron. 15:28; 16:42; 25:1,3,6; 2 Chron. 5:13,14; 34:12; Ps. 33:3).
- When you fall prostrate (to fall down flat in homage to royalty or God), you portray deep emotion and total surrender to God (see Ps. 72:11; Isa. 45:14).
- When you kneel, you are portraying humility and dependence upon God (see 2 Chron. 6:13; Matt. 17:14; Mark 1:40). Kneeling is asking for mercy (see Luke 22:41; Acts 9:40; 21:5).
- When you sit down or keep silent, you show forth rest and trust in God (see Exod. 14:14; Josh. 6:10; Job 2:13; Prov. 13:3; 17:27; Amos 5:13; Matt. 8:4; 12:16; 27:14; Luke 23:9; John 8:6).

The Word of God and Our Testimony: Our Foundation

Fasting and praising open up your spirit so you can effectively wield your most powerful weapon: the Word of God. This weapon is mentioned last, because it is the foundation upon which the entire arsenal rests. Everything you do in spiritual warfare must be based upon the Word of God.

The following verses vividly illustrate the fact that the Word of God is a military tool provided for Christian soldiers entering the spiritual battlefield:

And take...the sword of the Spirit, which is the word of God (Eph. 6:17).

For the word of God is living and active and sharper than any two-edged sword, and piercing as far as the division of soul and spirit, of both joints and marrow, and able to judge the thoughts and intentions of the heart (Heb. 4:12).

Words can either work for you or work against you. Learn to use them as Jesus did. It is His Word abiding in you that causes faith to be present in your words (see John 15:7,8). You can learn to use God's Word against the devil just as Jesus did when tempted by him. Jesus replied, "It is written...it is written...it is written." Each time He quoted God's Word, and He was the victor (see Matt. 4:4,7,10; 10:32).

When you confess God's Word aloud before others as your affirmation, Jesus confesses you before the Father (see Matt. 10:32). The more you know and confess the Word, the more effective the victory will be. Store Scripture in the reservoir of your spirit to use when needed.

A Document of Confirmation
Another effective way to use the Word as a weapon is to establish a "document of confirmation" based on the word the Lord has given for a particular situation. A document of confirmation is a most valuable weapon of spiritual warfare.

According to *Webster's Dictionary*, a document is "a lesson, a proof, anything printed, written, relied upon to record or prove something. Anything serving as proof, to prove or support, as by reference to documents."

Let's look at some documents in the Bible:

God told Moses on Mount Sinai to document His words to Israel by writing them on tablets. God considered them so important that when Moses later broke them, God immediately rewrote them with His finger. These we refer to as the Ten Commandments.

Then the Lord said to Moses, "Write down these words, for in accordance with these words I have made a covenant with you and with Israel" (Exod. 34:27).

When His people returned from captivity to Jerusalem, Nehemiah commanded them to renew their covenant relationship with God. "Now because of all this we are making an agreement in writing; and on the sealed document are the names of our leaders, our Levites and our priests" (Neh. 9:38).

God told Ezekiel to write a document of war, revealing to Ezekiel the heart of King Nebuchadnezzar to launch an all-out attack against Jerusalem. God instructed Ezekiel to mark the date down so that he would know later what God had told him was the truth:

> And the word of the Lord came to me in the ninth year, in the tenth month, on the tenth of the month, saying, "Son of man, write the name of the day, this very day. The king of Babylon has laid siege to Jerusalem this very day" (Ezek. 24:1,2).

The prophet Habakkuk was commanded by the Lord to record the vision which had been given him as a witness in the end time:

> Then the Lord answered me and said, "Record the vision and inscribe it on tablets, that the one who reads it may run. For the vision is yet for the appointed time; it hastens toward the goal, and it will not fail. Though it tarries, wait for it; for it will certainly come, it will not delay" (Hab. 2:2,3).

A document of confirmation is an article in writing that gives a word of testimony or promise, and usually has a date and a signature.

Many intercessors have found it helpful to keep a prayer journal to record words they receive from the Lord during their prayer time. God holds these words in high esteem; He will stand behind them to bring them to pass if they are in line with His Word and will. (See "Journaling: Recording What You Hear," chapter 6.)

A document of confirmation can be a passage of Scripture that He quickens to your spirit during your fellowship with Him. It can also be a direct word from the Lord revealed through a prophecy by the Holy Spirit. It may even be something the Lord reveals as He allows you to interpret what you have prayed in the Spirit. It will *always* be in alignment with God's Word, and consistent with God's character.

However you receive a word, write down the declaration and record the date. Later you will be blessed when remembering how God gave you the miracle He promised, or when you see the word come to pass.

Use your sword of the Spirit in the following ways:

1. Quote the Word to the enemy to remind him of his defeat.
2. Quote the Word to the Lord to affirm His promises that you are claiming on someone's behalf.
3. Ask the Lord to give you a word for direction for the person or situation for which you are interceding. (Example: In praying for someone with a serious illness, the Lord may give a word with a verse such as, "This sickness is not unto death" [John 11:4, *KJV*]. Then write it down and remain steadfast in prayer until the answer comes.)
4. Allow the Holy Spirit to quicken the Word to you for encouragement and correction, and to give guidance and strategy for your intercession.

The Names of God: Our Covenant

The Word of God admonishes all His people to "call upon His name." To do this more effectively, it helps to understand His attributes.

The next few pages are notes taken from *Names of God* by Nathan J. Stone. You will have a better understanding of God's character and will by knowing the provisions He has made for you through the power of His names. May your prayer life be enriched as you begin to refer to Him by some of the mighty names that follow:

ELOHIM:
Triune creator; sovereign of the universe, and life, and of all nations; who covenants to preserve His creation.

General idea of greatness, glory, creative and governing power, omnipotence, sovereignty, creator of the universe.

Elohim is mainly concerned with the *creation* and preservation of the world and His works. He assumes a great love toward all creation and creatures as the work of His hands.

Plural, representing the Trinity, under obligation of an oath to perform certain conditions.

EL:

Mighty, strong, prominent, "God," great, dreadful, "Almighty God."

EL SHADDAI:

The God who is "all-sufficient" and "all-bountiful," the One who fills and makes fruitful, used in connection with judging, chastening, purging, translated "almighty."

EL SHADDAI first appears in connection with Abraham in Genesis 17:1 *(KJV)*: "And when Abram was ninety years old and nine, Jehovah appeared to Abram, and said unto him, 'I am EL SHADDAI (God Almighty!)'" At this time Abram's name was changed to Abraham because he understood the revelation of EL SHADDAI as the One with whom all things were possible.

ADONI:

Sovereign Lord, master of our lives, sir, owner. Implies a claim upon man's obedience and service.

ADONI reveals the relationship which God sustains toward us and what He expects of us. ADONI is used hundreds of times in relation to Jesus Himself. We are not our own; we have been bought with a price. We belong to ADONI: spirit, soul, and body.

ADONI also represents the One who bestows gifts upon and equips His servants for service. We His servants are to be His inheritance, the portion and possession of His people.

JEHOVAH:

The being who is absolutely self-existent, possesses eternal life and permanent existence, eternal and unchangeable, the self-existent God of revelation.

JEHOVAH is known as the God who expresses Himself in essential moral and spiritual attributes. JEHOVAH reveals His love as conditioned upon moral and spiritual attributes. JEHOVAH places man under moral obligations with a warning of punishment for disobedience.

JEHOVAH is derived from the Hebrew verb *hayah* meaning "to be" or "being." It is the name most frequently employed in the Old Testament, occurring 6,519 times.

There are eight compound names of JEHOVAH in the Old Testament. *These names were used when JEHOVAH wanted to make a special revelation of Himself.*

1. JEHOVAH-JIREH (ji´ ra)
   "Jehovah's provision shall be seen"
2. JEHOVAH-RAPHA (rä´ fa)
   "Jehovah heals"
3. JEHOVAH-NISSI (nis´ se)
   "Jehovah my banner"
4. JEHOVAH-MEKADDISH (ma ka dish´)
   "Jehovah who sanctifies"
5. JEHOVAH-SHALOM (sha lom´)
   "Jehovah is peace"
6. JEHOVAH-TSIDKENU (tsid ka´ nu)
   "Jehovah our righteousness"
7. JEHOVAH-SHAMMAH (shäm mah´)
   "Jehovah is there"
8. JEHOVAH-ROHI (ro e´)
   "Jehovah my shepherd"

There is a wonderful and significant order in these compound names of JEHOVAH as they appear in Scripture. There is a progressive revelation of Jehovah providing for each need as it arises—saving, sustaining, strengthening, sanctifying. The order in which these eight names appear shows JEHOVAH'S purpose to meet the developing spiritual and physical needs of His people, Israel.

JEHOVAH-JIREH:
"Jehovah's provision shall be seen"

And Abraham said, "God will provide for Himself the lamb for the burnt offering, my son." So the two of them walked on together. ...And Abraham called the name of that place The Lord Will Provide, as it is said to this day, "In the mount of the Lord it will be provided" (Gen. 22:8,14).

MEANING: It shall be seen, it shall be provided; sense of fore-seeing, seer, prophet.

JEHOVAH-JIREH is a kind of seeing that is different from Elohim, all knowing. This kind of seeing means *foreseeing is prevision*. Prevision is the noun form of "seeing beforehand." Thus to God, prevision is followed with provision. FOR HE WILL CERTAINLY PROVIDE FOR THAT NEED WHICH HIS FORE-SEEING SHOWS TO EXIST. With Him prevision and provision are one and the same thing.

The name JEHOVAH-JIREH arose out of the instance of Jehovah's provision of a substitute for Isaac, whom He had commanded Abraham to sacrifice upon the altar. The name stands for *Jehovah's great provision for man's redemption in the sacrifice of His only begotton Son, Jesus.* He is the Lamb of God who takes away the sin of the world, who was offered up on the very spot where Abraham had predicted—"in the mount of the Lord it will be provided."

JEHOVAH-JIREH is to us the one who provides the sacrificial Lamb of God for our redemption.

JEHOVAH-RAPHA:
"Jehovah heals"

Then Moses led Israel from the Red Sea, and they went out into the wilderness of Shur; and they went three days in the wilderness and found no water. And when they came to Marah, they could not drink the waters of Marah, for they were bitter; therefore, it was named Marah. So the people grumbled at Moses, saying, "What shall we drink?"

Then he cried out to the Lord, and the Lord showed him a tree; and he threw it into the waters, and the waters became sweet. There He made for them a statute and regulation, and there He tested them. And He said, "If you will give earnest heed to the voice of the Lord your God, and do what is right in His sight, and give ear to His commandments, and keep all His statutes, I will put none of the diseases on you which I have put on the Egyptians; for I, the Lord, am your healer" (Exod. 15:22-26).

MEANING: To restore, to heal, to cure in a physical and spiritual sense.

The Lord Jesus consummated His ministry by becoming THE TREE that made the bitter pools of human existence waters of life. The teaching of Marah is wonderfully fulfilled in Him. *Jesus is both the tree and the waters.* He bore our sins in His body on the tree, and is also our Well of Salvation. Only Jesus, the tree of God's provision, purifies, sweetens, and heals man's bitter experiences in life. He heals the diseases of the soul and of the body.

JEHOVAH-NISSI:
"Jehovah my banner"

And Joshua did as Moses told him, and fought against Amalek; and Moses, Aaron, and Hur went up to the top of the hill. So it came about when Moses held his hand up, that Israel prevailed, and when he let his hand down, Amalek prevailed. But Moses' hands were heavy. Then they took a stone and put it under him, and he sat on it; and Aaron and Hur supported his hands, one on one side and one on the other. Thus his hands were steady until the sun set. So Joshua overwhelmed Amalek and his people with the edge of the sword. Then the Lord said to Moses, "Write this in a book as a memorial, and recite it to Joshua, that I will utterly blot out the memory of Amalek from under heaven." And Moses built an altar, and named it The Lord is My Banner; and he said, "The Lord has sworn; the Lord will have war against Amalek from generation to generation" (Exod. 17:10-16).

MEANING: The Lord our Banner, a sign of deliverance and salvation, the standard of our victory in life's conflicts.

A banner is translated: pole, ensign, standard; among the Jews it is a word associated with miracle.

It was a sign to God's people to rally to Him. The banner stood for His cause, His battle.

The banner of Jehovah held aloft in Moses' upraised hands brought victory to His people. This is always assured to the people of God—victory over the powers of evil, the enemy of our souls—when His banner is over us.

Isaiah predicts a rod to come forth out of the stem of Jesse. This stem or root is also a sign, a banner to the people. The stem of Jesse is Jesus, born of the seed of David according to the flesh. Jesus is our banner of redemption, our banner of welfare.

With Jehovah-Jesus as our banner, we may go from strength to strength giving thanks to God, "who always leads us in His triumph in Christ Jesus" (2 Cor. 2:14).

JEHOVAH-MAKADDISH:
"Jehovah who sanctifies"

You shall consecrate yourselves therefore and be holy, for I am the Lord your God. And you shall keep My statutes and practice them; *I am the Lord who sanctifies you* (Lev. 20:7,8).

MEANING: To set apart, sanctify or hallow, to dedicate, to consecrate, to be holy.

The book of Leviticus explains how a redeemed people should walk worthy of their calling and participate in the spiritual worship that Jehovah demands of them. In connection with Israel's moral and spiritual purity, this title, JEHOVAH-MAKADDISH, is repeated many times in Leviticus.

In the Old Testament the word "sanctify" was used to set apart places, furnishings, people and special days. The people of Israel were set apart to God and separated from all other people.

Jesus was from His very conception set apart by the power of the Holy Spirit. He was altogether holy, spotless and without sin.

Jesus became our High Priest, and in His redeeming love, He was made sin for us (see Luke 1:35; 2 Cor. 5:21; Heb. 4:15; 7:26).

Jesus became our Sanctification (see 1 Cor. 1:30; Heb. 10:10,14).

To such holiness, or separateness, we have been elected (see Eph. 1:4). Holiness is a positive and active word. The people of God must be holy in practice as well as separated in position. One is meaningless without the other. It is the Church's glorious destiny to be presented holy and spotless to her Lord.

JEHOVAH-SHALOM:
"Jehovah is peace"

When Gideon saw that he was the angel of the Lord, he said, "Alas, O Lord God! For now I have seen the angel of the Lord face to face." And the Lord said to him, "Peace to you, do not fear; you shall not die." Then Gideon built an altar there to the Lord and named it The Lord is Peace. To this day it is still in Ophrah of the Abiezrites (Judg. 6:22-24).

MEANING: Peace, wholeness, finished, making good a loss, welfare, well-being, perfect, deepest desire of the human heart. In the Hebrew language it also means harmony of relationship or a reconciliation based on the completion of a transaction, the payment of a debt, the giving of satisfaction.

PEACE OFFERING: A sacrifice, the shed blood of which provided atonement on which reconciliation and peace were based (see Lev. 3; 7:11-21). Peace is broken by sin. Peace offerings restored fellowship between God and man.

Jesus is the Prince of Peace who was promised to us in the Old Testament. While on earth, Jesus preached and promised peace. He healed, comforted and commanded the people to go in peace.

Jesus made peace for us through the blood of the cross. Our peace in Him is measured by our ability to keep trusting Him and by our sanctification. Peace depends on trust and obedience. If we are carnally minded we will lack peace. Therefore, let us allow peace to rule in our hearts (see Phil. 4:7,9; Col. 1:20; 3:15). There is no peace apart from Jesus, for individuals or for nations.

JEHOVAH-TSIDKENU:
"Jehovah our righteousness"

Behold, the days are coming, declares the Lord, when I shall raise up for David a righteous Branch; and He will reign as king and act wisely and do justice and righteousness in the land. In His days Judah will be saved, and Israel will dwell securely; and this is His name by which He will be called, "The Lord our Righteousness" (Jer. 23:5,6).

MEANING: Rendering justice and making right; to justify, declare innocent, or to acquit.

TSEDEK: This literal application of the word has to do with full weights or measures; from this idea is derived the meanings right toward God; righteousness and justice.

Israel was commanded to walk in the paths of righteousness and to offer the sacrifices of righteousness, putting their trust in the Lord. Jehovah, who is perfectly righteous, cannot overlook the lack of righteousness in man, for "He will by no means clear the guilty" (Num. 14:18).

It was prophesied by Isaiah that "in the Lord shall all the seed of Israel be justified" (Isa. 45:25). Jesus is that righteousness for both the Jews and the Gentiles; it is bestowed upon us as a free gift through faith.

JEHOVAH-TSIDKENU reveals to us the method and the measure of our acceptance before God, cleansed in the blood of the Lamb and clothed with the white robe of the righteousness of Him who is Jehovah-Jesus.

JEHOVAH-SHAMMAH:
"Jehovah is there"

The city shall be 18,000 cubits round about; and the name of the city from that day shall be, "The Lord is there" (Ezek. 48:35).

MEANING: The Lord is present, the Lord is there; His fullness dwells among us, He tabernacles with us, His glory is manifested among us.

JEHOVAH-SHAMMAH is the promise and pledge of the completion of that purpose in man's final rest and glory. For man's end is to glorify God and enjoy Him forever.

Ezekiel's prophecy of hope and consolation predicts the restoration of the land and people in a measure far beyond anything they had ever experienced in the past, or could have imagined.

The uniqueness of Israel had always been that the presence of God dwelled with them. The condition of His continued presence among them was their faithfulness to a covenant, by which they promised to be a holy people to a holy God.

The fullness of Jehovah's presence is our hope and end of all prophetic expectation, for we are both waiting and longing for His appearing. We are looking for the new heaven and the new earth where His righteousness will dwell with us forever.

JEHOVAH-ROHI:
"Jehovah my shepherd"

The Lord is my shepherd, I shall not want (Ps. 23:1).

MEANING: Companion, friend, to cherish, to feed or lead, to guide and direct and instruct.

The title SHEPHERD shows us that God is able to condescend to a relationship with mortal, sinful creatures whom He has redeemed. It suggests a one-on-one relationship to feed us and keep us as His inheritance (see 2 Sam. 7:8; Ps. 78:70-72).

Shepherding has not changed much in Palestine. A Palestinian shepherd lives with his animals night and day, establishing true intimacy with them. He calls each one by name, and they, knowing his voice and responding *only* to his call, follow him. By sleeping in the makeshift sheepfold, he protects the sheep from thieves and from preying animals who would devour them at night. The sheep sense his watchfulness and fear no evil. He provides pasture and water for them even in the wilderness.

If there can exist such a tender intimacy between a man and his sheep, how much more so between Jehovah and man, whom He Himself created? What a marvelous thing that God should offer Himself in such a relationship.

This portrays how we are in the shadow of our Father's loving care, watchful protection and strong defense. He truly keeps us from all evil. He never slumbers nor sleeps. He is attached and devoted to us and protects our lives from perils and pitfalls.

God is an intensely personal Shepherd. He knows each one of us individually.

Jesus is our Good Shepherd who came to gently lead us. He qualified Himself to become the Great Shepherd by first becoming a lamb, thus entering intimately into every experience and need of a sheep.[2]

Call Upon the Lord

You are now equipped to call upon the name that is above every name with the full assurance that He will give you everything you need to win the war and change the world for His glory. Take off the spirit of the world; put on your spiritual armor and get ready to fight. It's time to pray!

Notes

1. Arthur Wallis, *God's Chosen Fast* (Fort Washington, Pa.: Christian Literature Crusade, 1968). Permission granted. Adapted.
2. Nathan J. Stone, *Names of God* (Chicago: Moody, 1944).

Section V

A Guide
to Prayer

10

Daily Prayers

Guidelines for Daily Use

This section was originally written for those who intercede for missionaries, ministers and spiritual leaders, and who participate in the Intercessors International Prayer Ministry. These prayers do not have to be limited to leaders, but are easily adapted for your church, family or friends.

Topics for prayer have been provided for each day of the week. These prayers will meet the needs of those who are beginning their prayer journeys, those who feel they need a little extra help, and experienced intercessors. You may use any or all of these options; use the system that is most comfortable for you.

Each day of the week has a different emphasis. For example, look at Sunday:

1. If prayer is a way of life for you, select the subject "Favor with God" and pray as the Spirit of the Lord directs you.
2. If you would like more guidance, an outline is provided with subtopics such as "Favor with God," "Spiritual Revelation," "Anointing" and "Holiness." Use each item as you pray.
3. Whether experienced or inexperienced, you will find value in the Scripture-based written prayers. Using these prayers, insert the name(s) of the person(s) you

are praying for. For instance, the subtopic "Revelation": "Father, I ask that You give to (Pastor Paul and Ruth) Your spirit of wisdom and revelation in the deep, intimate and full knowledge of You, the eyes of their hearts and understanding being enlightened...." *The written prayers are a guide, not a formula.* Allow the Holy Spirit to lead you in the way He desires to pray through you.

As you pray, you may add additional Scriptures relating to the daily topics and subtopics. You may want to note them in your prayer journal, or write them out as they become a part of your Scripture praying.

We encourage you to pray the topics each day as we have written. The "Daily Prayers" section has been developed for this purpose—to maintain a daily theme so that each intercessor will be in unity and harmony with other pray-ers around the world. With each of us united and intent on one purpose, we will pull down the strongholds of the enemy, and our leaders will walk in victory.

Remember your work ahead is going to be challenging and constant. Yes, intercession is *work, but it has heavenly rewards.*

Weekly Schedule and Topics for Daily Prayers

Sunday: Psalm 90:17
Favor with God
Monday: Acts 2:47
Favor with Man
Tuesday: Habakkuk 2:2
Pure Vision
Wednesday: 1 Thessalonians 5:23
Spirit, Soul, Body
Thursday: Psalm 91
Warfare and Protection
Friday: Matthew 6:33
Priorities
Saturday: Ephesians 5:33-6:4
Family

SUNDAY
Favor with God

I. Favor with God
Pray:

1. For leaders to walk in the Spirit, pleasing to the Lord.
2. For leaders to serve the Lord with reverent fear, and rejoice with trembling. (See Ps. 2:10,11.)
3. For leaders to be willing to obey God's direction.
4. For leaders to maintain a teachable spirit.

II. Spiritual Revelation
Pray:

1. For the Holy Spirit to give personal direction, teaching and vision.
2. For ever-increasing knowledge of God.
3. For revelation of the depths of God and spiritual knowledge of the Word of God.

III. Anointing
Pray:

1. For leaders' work to be of good quality—the best.
2. For leaders to have strength to withstand fiery tests.
3. For leaders to have the sevenfold *Spirit of the Lord*; for the Spirit of the Lord, and the spirits of wisdom, under-standing, counsel, strength, knowledge and reverent fear of the Lord to rest upon them.
4. For leaders to be strengthened with power in the inner man.
5. For leaders to be sensitive to God's voice—spiritual ears and heart.
6. For leaders to speak the Word with boldness wherever they go.

7. For gifts of the Spirit to flow through leaders: words of wisdom and knowledge, faith, healing, working of miracles, prophecy, distinguishing of spirits, tongues and interpretation of tongues.

8. For leaders to be full of mercy and compassion, walking in forgiveness; enabled to counsel others with God's mercy, grace.

9. For leaders to speak and preach with such an anointing from the Spirit of God that all unsaved who hear will come to a saving knowledge of Jesus Christ as Lord.

IV. Holiness
Pray:

1. Bind all principalities and powers assigned to hinder leaders' place of abiding with God in devotional time.

2. For leaders to set aside ample time for prayer and fellowship with the Lord in a productive, personal manner.

3. For leaders to know the depths of God's love; to be grounded in love.

4. For leaders to be sensitive to the Father's heart.

5. For leaders to be good stewards of gifts, talents, time and money.

6. For leaders to live lives of faith and trust in the Lord.

7. For leaders to let Jesus be glorified in their lives—be good role models.

8. For leaders to walk in holiness.

Sunday Prayer
Father, in Jesus' name, I come boldly and with confidence to the throne of grace to obtain mercy and receive grace to help in time of need for (names). (See Heb. 4:16.)

Revelation
Father, I ask that You give to (names) Your spirit of wisdom and revelation in the deep, intimate, full knowledge of

You, the eyes of their hearts and understanding being enlightened and flooded with light, that they might know what is the hope of their calling, and what are the riches of the glory of Your inheritance in them, and what is the exceeding greatness of Your power toward them, because they do believe according to the working of Your mighty power which You wrought in Christ, when You raised Him from the dead, and set Him at Your own right hand in the heavenly places. (See Eph. 1:17-20.)

And Father, even as Your servant Moses was faithful in all Your house, and You spoke to him face-to-face, even so I pray that (names) will be faithful and entrusted in all Your house, and that You would speak face-to-face, and mouth-to-mouth with them—openly, clearly and directly, and not in dark sayings or riddles. (See Num. 12:7,8.)

I pray (names) will keep and obey Your commandments and words so that they may continue to abide in Your love, so that You will come unto them and make Your abode and special dwelling place with them, and love them, and show and reveal and manifest Yourself to them, and make Yourself real and be clearly seen by them. (See John 15:9,10; 14:21,23.)

Anointing

Father, I ask that the Spirit of the Lord rest upon (names)— the spirit of wisdom and understanding, the spirit of counsel and might and strength, the spirit of knowledge and of the reverential and obedient fear of the Lord. (See Isa. 11:2.)

I pray (names) will not be vague or thoughtless or foolish, but will be understanding, firmly grasping the will of the Lord; that they may ever be continually filled with the Holy Spirit, and with the fruit that the Holy Spirit produces: love, joy, peace, patience, kindness, goodness, faithfulness, gentleness and self-control. I pray that (names) walk and live habitually in the Holy Spirit, responsive to, controlled and guided and led by the Holy

Spirit, so that they will not gratify or carry out the cravings and desires of the flesh, and not be subject to, or come under the law. (See Eph. 5:17,18; Gal. 5:22,23; 5:16,18.)

Father, grant that the manifestation of the Spirit be given to (names) to profit them in all they do: the word of wisdom, the word of knowledge, faith, gifts of healing, the working of miracles, prophecy, discerning of spirits, kinds of tongues and the interpretation of tongues. (See 1 Cor. 12:7-10.)

I pray these attesting signs will accompany (names) because they believe: In Your name (names) will drive out demons; they will speak in new languages; if they pick up serpents or drink anything deadly, it will not hurt them; (names) will lay their hands on the sick, and they will get well. (See Mark 16:17,18.)

And, Father, I pray that as (names) go out and preach everywhere, You will keep working with them, and keep confirming the message by the attesting signs and miracles that closely accompany the message. (See Mark 16:20.)

Father, I pray that (name)'s speech and their preaching not be set forth in persuasive, enticing and plausible words of man's wisdom, but in demonstration of the Holy Spirit and power, that is a proof by Your Spirit and power operating through them and stirring in the minds of their listeners and hearers, the most holy emotions, and thus, persuading them, so that their faith might not rest in the wisdom of men or in human philosophy, but in the power of God. (See 1 Cor. 2:4,5.)

Father, I pray that (names) retain the standard of sound words, in the faith and love which are in Christ Jesus, and that You open up to them a door for the Word, so they may speak forth the mystery of Christ, in order that they may make it clear in the way they ought to speak, and that their speech always be with grace, seasoned with salt, so they may know how to respond to each person. (See 2 Tim. 1:13; Col. 4:3,4,6.)

Holiness

And, Father, like the Holy One who called them is holy, I pray that (names) may be holy also in all their behavior. (See 1 Pet. 1:15,16.)

I ask that (names) may be filled with the knowledge of Your will in all spiritual wisdom and understanding, so that they may walk in a manner worthy of the Lord, to please You in all respects, bearing fruit in every good work and increasing in the knowledge of God, strengthened with all power, according to Your glorious might, for the attaining of all steadfastness and patience. (See Col. 1:9-11.)

I pray that You will instruct (names) and teach them in the way they should go, and counsel them with Your eye upon them. (See Ps. 32:8.)

Favor with God

I pray that (names) will trust in You, in order that lovingkindness and mercy may surround them. That they will not trust in people or make flesh their strength, but trust in the Lord that they may be blessed. (See Ps. 32:10; Jer. 17:5,7.)

I pray (names) will continue in the faith firmly established, grounded and settled, and steadfast, and not be moved away from the hope of the gospel. (See Col. 1:23.)

I pray they will abide vitally united to You, and that Your words will remain in and continue to live in their hearts, so that (names) may ask whatever they will and it shall be done for them. For You have called and chosen them that they might go and bring forth much fruit, and keep on bearing lasting, remaining, abiding fruit, that You may be honored and glorified, and that (names) may show and prove themselves to be true followers and disciples of Yours. (See John 15:7,16,8.)

I pray, Father, that (names) continue building themselves up on their most holy faith, praying in the Holy Spirit, keeping themselves in the love of God, and looking for the mercy of our Lord Jesus Christ unto eternal life. (See Jude 20,21.)

Now to Him, who is able to establish (names) according to the gospel and the preaching of Jesus Christ, according to the revelation of the mystery which has been kept secret for long ages past, but now is manifested, and by the Scriptures of the prophets, according to the commandment of the eternal God, which has been made known to all the nations, leading to obedience of faith; now to the only wise God, through Jesus Christ, be the glory forever. Amen. (See Rom. 16:25-27.)

Monday

Favor with Man

I. Congregation and All Who Receive Ministry from Leaders
Pray:

1. That they have teachable spirits and open hearts.
2. That they grow up to be wise and strong.
3. That they be supportive and responsive to leaders with love, prayers, encouragement, finances.
4. That all deluding influences be kept away from them.
5. That they not be followers of "tradition."
6. That they be open to new moves of the Holy Spirit.
7. That they be sensitive to financial needs of the spiritual leaders and ministry, and support them.
8. That gossip, deceit and unbelief be kept away.
9. That revival spring forth in their lives, church, community, state and nation.
10. That God send His ministering angels to guard them.

II. Ministry Staff
Pray:

1. That they be in unity and tuned to the Holy Spirit for direction—be supportive of one another.

2. That they esteem one another more highly than themselves.
3. That they communicate clearly, and not be misunderstood.
4. That no weapon formed against them shall prosper.
5. That they work together well as a team.
6. That they each be honest in their relationships with one another.
7. That they be faithful in commitment to one another and congregation or ministry.

III. Leaders' Relationship with the Staff
Pray:

1. That they communicate clearly and not be misunderstood.
2. That they be able to impart the "vision" God has given them to other staff members.
3. That they relate well to each one on an individual basis with much wisdom, understanding and sensitivity.
4. That God give them the needed anointing for their jobs.
5. That they be peacemakers.
6. That God give them a spirit of wisdom, understanding, knowledge, counsel, strength, and obedient and reverent fear of the Lord. (See Isa. 11:2.)
7. That each one complete the work given him/her to do.

IV. Unsaved
Pray:

1. That the leaders witness effectively and boldly to the lost.
2. That God prepare the hearts of those with whom they will share the gospel.
3. That the people they preach or witness to be saved and filled with the Holy Spirit.
4. That Satan not snatch away the Word that has been planted in their hearts.

V. Government

Pray:

1. For wisdom and direction for government leaders in the nations.
2. For them to know that they are in the hands of the Lord and He turns them wherever He wishes. (See Prov. 21:1.)
3. For their hearts to be open to receive the Word of God, salvation in Jesus Christ alone.
4. For laws of their nation to be established on honest biblical principles.
5. For the eyes of their understanding to be opened to truth in God's Word.
6. For revival to sweep through the government offices and no seed planted be stolen.
7. Bind all violence and antichrist spirits over the government agencies.
8. Bind away the powers of the enemy, keeping them from hearing and responding to the gospel. Loose them from false gods, ancestral traditions and any other influences or spirits that keep them from receiving the full gospel of Jesus Christ.

Monday Prayer
Government

Father, in Jesus' name, I come to pray first for leaders and all who are in authority in the countries where (names) live and minister, in order that they may lead a quiet and tranquil and peaceable life in all godliness and dignity and honesty. For this is good and acceptable in Your sight, for You desire all people to be saved and to come to the knowledge of the truth. (See 1 Tim. 2:1-4.)

I pray, Father, that these rulers in authority in (name of country) be not a terror to good works, but to the evil; that these rulers be Your ministers and bring just punishment to those who do evil. (See Rom. 13:3.)

Give these leaders knowledge of Your way of judging, O God, and give them the Spirit of Your righteousness to control all their actions. Let them judge and govern Your people with righteousness, and Your poor and afflicted with judgment and justice. I pray the mountains bring peace to the people, and the hills, through the general establishment of righteousness. May these leaders judge and defend the poor of the people, deliver the children of the needy, and crush the oppressor so all may revere and fear You while the sun and moon endure, throughout all generations. (See Ps. 72:1-5.)

I pray these leaders in authority will deliver the needy when they call, the poor also and the person who has no helper; that the leaders will have pity on the poor and weak and needy, and that they will save the lives of the needy, and redeem their lives from oppression and fraud and violence. I pray also that precious and costly shall be the blood of the needy in Your sight and in the sight of the leaders. (See Ps. 72:12-14.)

I pray that prayer shall be made for the needy continually, and that men shall be blessed by these leaders and that all nations shall call them and You blessed. (See Ps. 72:15,17.)

Father, I pray that You take away the wicked from before these leaders in authority in (name of country) so their government will be established in righteousness. For promotion comes not from the east, nor from the west, nor from the south, but You are judge. You put down one and lift up another. I pray they may be surrounded with many wise and righteous counselors who love peace. (See Prov. 25:5; Ps. 75:6,7; Prov. 12:20.)

I pray, Father, that these leaders in authority will not crave strong drink nor wine, lest they drink and forget the law, and pervert the judgment of any of the afflicted. I pray they will not receive a bribe from the bosom to pervert the ways of justice, but that they will give stability to the land by justice, and not take a bribe to overthrow it. (See Prov. 31:4,5; 17:23; 29:4.)

Lord, counsel is Yours, and sound wisdom. You are understanding, and power is Yours. By You kings reign, and rulers decree justice. By You princes rule, and nobles, and all who judge rightly. I pray these rulers in authority will diligently seek You so that they may find You. (See Prov. 8:14-17.)

Those Not Saved

Father, having overlooked the times of ignorance, You are now declaring to men that all men everywhere should repent, because You have fixed a day in which You will judge the world in righteousness, through Jesus Christ whom You have appointed, having furnished proof to all men by raising Him from the dead. (See Acts 17:30,31.)

Father, You are not slow about Your promise, as some count slowness, but You are patient toward us, not wishing for any to perish, but for all to come to repentance. For the Son of Man has come to seek, and to save that which was lost, and You said, "I will have mercy, and not sacrifice: For I am not come to call the righteous, but sinners to repentance." (See 2 Pet. 3:9; Luke 19:10; Matt. 9:13.)

Lord, according to Your Word, I am asking for the unreached peoples to be an inheritance for (names), and the uttermost parts of the earth for their possession. (See Ps. 2:8.)

Father, I ask that You grant sinners, who will be ministered to by (names), repentance from dead works, and faith toward God. That these sinners put aside all filthiness and all that remains of wickedness. And I pray that they receive in humility the engrafted Word, which is able to save their souls. (See Heb. 6:1; Jas. 1:21.)

I ask that You pour out on sinners, who will be ministered to by (names), Your Spirit of grace and supplication so they can look on Jesus, whom they have pierced. I ask that Your Spirit of truth come and convict them concerning sin, righteousness and judgment. Convict sinners concerning sin because they do not believe in Jesus; convict sinners concerning righteousness because Jesus went back to You; and convict sinners concerning judgment because the ruler of this world has been judged. (See Zech. 12:10; John 16:8-11,13.)

Thank You, Father, You are able to save forever those who draw near to You through Jesus, since He always lives to make intercession for them. I pray these sinners receive Your Spirit of adoption as sons, by which they may cry out, "ABBA! Father!" I pray the Holy Spirit, Himself, will bear witness with their spirit, and that they become the children of God. (See Heb. 7:25; Rom. 8:15,16.)

Those Needing Ministry

I pray, Father, that You open a door for the Word, so (names) may speak forth the mystery of Christ; and that they may make it clear in the way they ought to speak. (See Col. 4:3,4.)

I pray (names) would conduct themselves with wisdom toward outsiders, making the most of their opportunities and using their time wisely. I pray their speech be always with grace, seasoned, as it were, with salt, so that they may know how to respond to each person. (See Col. 4:5,6.)

I pray, Father, that those receiving ministry continue in the faith firmly established and steadfast, grounded and settled, and that they not be moved away from the hope of the gospel which they have heard. Sanctify them in Your truth; Your Word is truth. (See Col. 1:23; John 17:17.)

May the Word of the Lord spread rapidly and be glorified. May (names), as well as those receiving ministry, be delivered from perverse and evil men, for not all have faith. Thank You, Father, that because You are faithful, You will strengthen them and protect them from the evil one. (See 2 Thess. 3:1-3.)

I pray that the hearts of those receiving ministry may be comforted and encouraged, being knit together in love, and attaining to all the wealth that comes from the full assurance of understanding, resulting in a true knowledge of Your mystery, that is Christ Himself, in whom are hidden all the treasures of wisdom and knowledge. (See Col. 2:2,3.)

Leadership and Staff

Holy Father, I thank You that no weapon formed against (names) or their coworkers, or their families, or their ministries shall prosper, and every tongue that has risen against them in judgment shall be shown to be in the wrong. For this peace, righteousness, security and triumph over opposition is the heritage of these servants of the Lord, and this is the righteousness and vindication which they obtain from You—that which You impart to them as their justification. (See Isa. 54:17.)

Since then, Father, (names) have been raised up with Christ to a new life, thus sharing Jesus' resurrection from the dead, I pray that they aim at and keep seeking the rich, eternal treasures that are above, where Christ is, seated at the right hand of God. That they set their minds and keep them set on what is above, the higher things, not on the things that are on the earth. For as far as this world is concerned, they have died and their new real life is hid with Christ in God. (See Col. 3:1-3.)

I pray that (names) be of the same mind, maintaining the same love, united in spirit, intent on one purpose. That they walk in a manner worthy of the calling with which they have been called, with all humility and gentleness, with patience, showing forbearance to one another in love, being diligent to preserve the unity of the Spirit in the bond of peace and forgiving one another, whoever has a complaint against any one, just as the Lord forgave them. May they give no cause for offense in anything, in order that the ministry be not discredited, but in everything commending themselves as servants of God. (See Phil. 2:2; Eph. 4:1-3; Col. 3:13; 2 Cor. 6:3,4.)

I pray that whatever these staff members do, they do their work heartily as for the Lord rather than for men, knowing that from the Lord they will receive the reward of the inheritance; for it is the Lord Christ whom they serve. (See Col. 3:23,24.)

Favor

For You, Lord, will bless the righteous. As with a shield You will surround (names) with goodwill, pleasure and favor. (See Ps. 5:12.)

Father, I pray Your servants will not forsake mercy and kindness and truth, but that they will shut out all hatred and selfishness and deliberate hypocrisy and falsehood. I pray (names) will bind mercy and kindness and truth about their necks, and write them on the tablet of their hearts, so that they may find favor, good understanding and high esteem in the sight and judgment of God and man. (See Prov. 3:3,4.)

Father, I pray that in all matters of wisdom and understanding, when (names) are consulted, that their counsel will be found to be ten times better than the counsel of all those in the whole country round about. (See Dan. 1:20.)

Tuesday
Pure Vision

I. Vision
Pray:

1. For God to clarify His vision for ministry to these leaders.
2. For patience until its fulfillment.
3. For finances for the vision to come forth.
4. For a "wall of fire" to protect the vision. (See Zech. 2:5.)
5. For helpers in carrying out the vision.
6. Do spiritual warfare against tactics of the enemy that would delay vision from coming forth in God's timing.

7. Stop the mouths of those who would speak against the vision.

II. Wisdom and Enlightenment
Pray:

1. For the Holy Spirit to continually give enlightenment and reveal hidden knowledge of the mysteries of Christ.
2. For keen discernment between God's wisdom and human wisdom.
3. For a teachable spirit.
4. For them to not depend on past experience or direction, but seek instead fresh wisdom and guidance before making any decision.

III. Motives
Pray:

1. For pure motives, purged by God through the Word and prayer time.
2. For awareness that God can give right motives.
3. For God to continually renew their thought lives and put a right spirit within.
4. For any wrong motives/thoughts done in darkness to be brought to light, and dealt with in a Christlike way.
5. For discernment against impure motives; for wisdom and knowledge on how to deal with them, and the discipline to do it.

IV. Guidance
Pray:

1. For dependence on God for guidance during prayer time and all during the day as decisions are made.
2. For right people to come into their lives at the right time to give godly counsel.
3. For God to lead and direct their paths.

Tuesday Prayer

Understanding

Father, in Jesus' name, I come before You making request with intercession for (names). Father, I thank You for these precious "love gifts" to the Body of Christ. (See Eph. 1:16; 4:8.)

Thank You, Father, that the Son of God has come, and has given (names) understanding, in order that they might know Him who is true. (See 1 John 5:20.)

Thank You, Father, that wisdom is in the presence of the one who has understanding, and that because (names) seek You, they can understand all things. For You give wisdom, and out of Your mouth comes knowledge and understanding. (See Prov. 17:24; 28:5; 2:6.)

I pray they may be of quick understanding, and that their delight be in the reverential and obedient fear of the Lord. May (names) not judge by what their eyes see, nor make a decision by what their ears hear; but with righteousness may they judge the poor, and decide with fairness for the afflicted of the earth. May they smite the earth and the oppressor with the rod of their mouths, and with the breath of their lips slay the wicked. May righteousness be the belt around their loins, and faithfulness the belt around their waists. (See Isa. 11:3-5.)

Wisdom

Thank You, Father, (names) have an anointing from the Holy One, and they know all things. (See 1 John 2:20.)

Thank You, Father, that by Your doing they are in Christ Jesus, who became to them wisdom from God, righteousness, sanctification and redemption. (See 1 Cor. 1:30.)

I pray, Father, that (names) will be wise and understanding, and show by their good behavior their deeds in the gentleness of wisdom that is from above: being first pure, then peaceable, gentle, reasonable, full of mercy and good fruits, unwavering, and without hypocrisy. And that the fruit of righteousness be sown in peace by (names), who make peace. (See Jas. 3:13,17,18.)

I pray that wisdom and knowledge shall be the stability of their times and strength of salvation; and that the fear of the Lord is their treasure. (See Isa. 33:6.)

Guidance

I pray (names) will trust in You, Lord, with all their hearts; and that they will not lean on their own understanding. I pray that in all their ways they will acknowledge You, and You will make their paths straight. For You, Father, lead the humble in justice, and teach the humble Your way. (See Prov. 3:5,6; Ps. 25:9.)

A man's way is not in himself; nor is it in a man who walks to direct his steps. The steps of (names) are ordered by You, Father, and You delight in their way. (See Ps. 37:23; Jer. 10:23.)

Make them to know Your ways, Father; teach them Your paths. Lead them in Your truth and teach them, for You are the God of their salvation; for You they wait all the day. (See Ps. 25:4,5.)

Thank You, Father, for You teach (names) to profit, and lead them in the way they should go. (See Isa. 48:17.)

Enlightenment

Lord of Glory, I pray that You might give to (names) Your spirit of wisdom and revelation in the sphere of a full knowledge of Yourself, with the eyes of their hearts being enlightened, knowing what is the hope of Your calling, what is the wealth of the glory of Your inheritance in them as saints, and what is the superabounding greatness of Your inherent power to them who are the believing ones, as measured by the operative energy of the manifested strength of Your might. (See Eph. 1:17-19.)

And, Father, I pray that You would make known to (names) the mystery of Your will according to Your good pleasure which You have purposed in Yourself. (See Eph. 1:9.)

Will of God and Vision

Father, I ask that You fill Your servants with a clear knowledge of Your will by giving them every kind of spiritual wisdom and understanding, so they might live worthy of the Lord, aiming to please You in every way as they produce every kind of good work, and grow by knowing You better. (See Col. 1:9,10.)

Father, I pray that You would count (names) worthy of this calling, and that they would fulfill every good pleasure of Your goodness, and the work of faith with power, in order that the name of our Lord Jesus may be glorified in them, and they in Him, according to the grace of our God and the Lord Jesus Christ. (See 2 Thess. 1:11,12.)

I pray (names) will intimately come to know and recognize, and listen to and heed, the voice of the Good Shepherd. For You call them by name and lead them out. I pray they follow You, because they know Your voice; that they will never on any account follow a stranger, but will run away from him, because they do not know the voice of strangers or recognize their call. (See John 10:3-5.)

Ministry

Precious Father, I pray that (names) might fully carry out the preaching of the Word of God; that is, the mystery which has been hidden from the past ages and generations; but which has now been manifested to Your saints, to whom You willed to make known what are the riches of the glory of this mystery among the Gentiles, which is Christ in them, the hope of glory. (See Col. 1:25b-27.)

And, Father, I pray that (names) will proclaim Christ, admonishing and teaching every man with all wisdom, that they may present every man complete in Christ, striving according to Your power, which mightily works within them. (See Col. 1:28,29.)

I ask that You give them utterance and wisdom which

none of their opponents will be able to resist or refute. (See Luke 21:15.)

Thoughts, Motives, Renewed Mind

Father, I pray (names) be not conformed to this world, but that they be transformed by the renewing of their minds, that they may prove what Your will is, that which is good and acceptable and perfect. That they pull down every stronghold, cast down every imagination and every high thing that exalts itself against the knowledge of God, and bring into captivity every thought to the obedience of Christ. (See Rom. 12:2; 2 Cor. 10:4,5.)

Father, whatever is true, whatever is honorable, whatever is right, whatever is pure, whatever is lovely, whatever is of good repute, if there is any excellence and if anything worthy of praise, may (names) let their minds dwell on these things. (See Phil. 4:8.)

Create in them a clean heart, Holy Father, and renew a steadfast spirit within them. Do not cast (names) away from Your presence, and do not take Your Holy Spirit from them. Restore to them the joy of Your salvation, and sustain them with a willing spirit. Then will they teach transgressors Your ways, and sinners will be converted to You. (See Ps. 51:10-13.)

WEDNESDAY
Spirit, Soul, Body

I. Health
Pray:

1. For divine health—physically, mentally, emotionally.
2. For all effects of tiredness and discouragement to be loosed from their bodies and minds.
3. For the leaders to recognize the need to care for their physical bodies with adequate rest.
4. For wisdom and self-control in eating (loosed from compulsion).

5. For time to exercise properly.
6. For adequate strength to accomplish tasks.

II. Appearance
Pray:

1. For leaders to maintain the glow of Jesus.
2. For leaders to attract others to the Lord through tidy appearance, right actions and gentle speech.

III. Attitudes
Pray:

1. For fruit of the Spirit. (See Gal. 5:22,23.)
2. For gracious but firm attitudes—to learn when/how to say no.
3. For mercy, compassion.
4. For desire to be a peacemaker and to restore broken relationships.
5. For total submission to the Lord in every area of life.
6. For a spirit of unity, not competition.
7. For humility rather than superiority.
8. For cooperation rather than defensiveness.
9. For discernment to recognize wrong attitudes in themselves, and courage to deal with them immediately.

IV. Spiritual and Physical Wholeness
Pray:

1. For leaders to pursue righteousness, faith, love and peace.
2. For leaders to refuse foolish and ignorant speculations.
3. For leaders to have a desire to go on with Jesus regardless of the cost involved.
4. For leaders to feed daily on the Word of God, meditating on God's precepts.
5. For leaders to commune with God daily in prayer.

Wednesday Prayer

Health

Thank You, Father, through Jesus Christ for (names); in Jesus' name I bring these requests and petitions before You on their behalf.

Thank You for sending Your Word, the Lord Jesus, and healing (names) and delivering them from their destructions. I give You thanks for Your loving-kindness, and for Your wonders to the sons of men. I pray they will also offer You sacrifices of thanksgiving, and tell of Your works with joyful singing. (See Ps. 107:20-22.)

Father, I pray that (names) give attention to Your words, and incline their ears to Your sayings; that they do not let them depart from their sight, and that they keep them in the midst of their hearts, because they are life to those who find them and health to their whole body. (See Prov. 4:20-22.)

Thank You, Father, that because (names) serve You, You will bless their bread and their water, and You will remove sickness from their midst. (See Exod. 23:25.)

Father, I pray their souls bless You, and that they not forget any of Your benefits: for You pardon all their iniquities; You heal all their diseases; You redeem their lives from the pit; You crown (names) with loving-kindness and compassion; You satisfy their years and desires with good things so that their youth is renewed like the eagle's; and You, only, perform righteous deeds, and judgments for all who are oppressed. (See Ps. 103:2-6.)

Father, thank You that the Spirit of Him who raised Jesus from the dead dwells in (names), and that because You raised Christ Jesus from the dead, You will also give life to their mortal bodies through Your Spirit who indwells them. (See Rom. 8:11.)

I thank You, Father, that Jesus, Himself, bore their sins in His own body on the cross, that they might die to sin and live to righteousness; for by His wounds they were healed. (See 1 Pet. 2:24.)

Thank You, Father, that Christ has redeemed (names) from the curse of the Law, having become a curse for them, for it is written, "Cursed is every one who hangs on a tree," in order that in Christ Jesus the blessing of Abraham might come to the Gentiles, that they might receive the promise of the Spirit through faith. Thank You, Father, (names) belong to Christ, and are Abraham's off-spring, and heirs according to promise. (See Gal. 3:13,14,29.)

Appearance

O, Father, Christ gave Himself up for (names), that He might sanctify and cleanse them with the washing of water by the Word, that He might present them to Himself, not having spot or wrinkle, or any such thing, but that they should be holy and without blemish. (See Eph. 5:25b-27.)

I pray, Father, that whatever (names) do in word or deed, they do it all in the name of the Lord Jesus, giving thanks through Him to You. (See Col. 3:17.)

Thank You, Father, (names) have put on righteous-ness, and it clothes them; their justice is like a robe and a turban. (See Job 29:14.)

I pray they be clothed with strength and dignity. I pray they also clothe themselves with humility toward one another, for You are opposed to the proud, but give grace to the humble. I pray (names) will humble themselves, there-fore, under Your mighty hand, that You may exalt them at the proper time; that they cast all their anxiety upon You, because You care for them. (See Prov. 31:25a; 1 Pet. 5:5b-7.)

I pray, Father, that no one look down on (names), but rather in speech, conduct, love, faith and purity, they will show themselves an example of those who believe. (See 1 Tim. 4:12.)

Father, I pray (names) will abstain from all appear-ance of evil. (See 1 Thess. 5:22.)

Spiritual and Physical Wholeness

I pray, Father, that (names) discipline themselves for the purpose of godliness; for bodily discipline is only of little profit, but godliness is profitable for all things, since it holds promise for the present life and also for the life to come. (See 1 Tim. 4:7,8.)

I pray (names) will glorify God in their bodies, for they have been bought with a price, and are not their own; for their bodies are a temple for the Holy Spirit. (See 1 Cor. 6:19,20.)

I pray they will not hurt or destroy the temple of God, for the temple of God is holy, and that is what they are. (See 1 Cor. 3:16,17.)

Thank You, Father, that (names) are a building being fitted together and growing into a holy temple in the Lord, in whom they also are being built together into a dwelling of God in the Spirit. (See Eph. 2:21,22.)

I pray, Father, that (names) cleanse themselves from wickedness, that they will be vessels for honor, sanctified and useful to You, prepared for every good work. I pray that they flee from youthful lusts, and pursue righteousness, faith, love and peace with those who call on the Lord from a pure heart. And that they refuse foolish and ignorant speculations, knowing they produce quarrels. (See 2 Tim. 2:21-23.)

Attitude

Thank You, Father, (names) have been called to freedom; only I pray they do not turn their freedom into an opportunity for the flesh, but through love may they serve one another. For the whole law is fulfilled in one word, in the statement, "You shall love your neighbor as yourself." (See Gal. 5:13,14.)

I pray, Father, that (names) forget what lies behind and reach forward to what lies ahead, pressing on toward the goal for the prize of the upward call of God in Christ Jesus. And if in anything they have a different attitude, Father, I pray You reveal it also to them. (See Phil. 3:13-15.)

So, Father, I pray (names) do nothing from selfishness or empty conceit, but with humility of mind let them regard one another as more important than themselves; that they do not merely look out for their own personal interests, but also for the interests of others. I pray they will have the same attitude in themselves which was also in Christ Jesus. (See Phil. 2:3-5.)

Blessings

Father, I pray that You bless (names), and keep them; that You make Your face to shine on them, and be gracious to them; that You lift up Your countenance upon them, and give them peace. (See Num. 6:24-26.)

Cause (names) to increase and abound in love for one another, and for all men, so that You may establish their hearts unblamable in holiness before You at the coming of our Lord Jesus with all Your saints. (See 1 Thess. 3:12,13.)

Father, I pray (names) will fear You and keep Your commandments, for this is the whole duty of man and what You require of them for their good: that they fear You; that they walk in all Your ways; that they love You, and serve You out of and with their whole hearts, and with all their souls, and with all their minds, their faculties of thought, of quick apprehension, intelligence, keenness of discernment, and moral understanding, and with all their strength. (See Mark 12:30,33; Eccles. 12:13; Deut. 10:12,13.)

THURSDAY
Warfare and Protection

I. Protection
Pray:

1. That God send angels to guard over missionaries, ministers, spiritual leaders, their families and property— make a hedge to guard all that is going in and coming out, the air above and the ground below.

2. That the angels go before them and do battle on the leaders' behalf. (Example: Michael, one of the chief princes, doing battle on Daniel's behalf.) (See Dan 10:13.)
3. That God foil all attacks and traps of the enemy and keep the leaders from the nets of the enemy while they walk by safely. (See Pss. 35; 37; 141:9,10.)
4. That God be the leaders' hiding place and preserve them from trouble, surrounding them with songs of deliverance. (See Ps. 32:7.)
5. For the leaders' protection. (See Ps. 91.)
6. That the Holy Spirit open the leaders' eyes to the plans, plots, ploys and traps of the enemy.
7. That the Holy Spirit go before them and make the crooked places straight and shatter the doors of bronze and cut through the bars of iron. (See Isa. 45:2.)

II. Temptation
Pray:

1. That the missionaries, ministers and spiritual leaders stand firm and not succumb to the difficult times of the last days—that they not be lovers of self, lovers of money, boastful, proud, abusive, disobedient to parents, ungrateful, unholy, without love, unforgiving, slanderous, without self-control, brutal, not lovers of good, treacherous, rash, conceited, lovers of pleasure rather than lovers of God. (See 2 Tim. 3:2-4.)
2. That the leaders not fall to the lust of the flesh, the lust of the eyes, nor the pride of life. (See 1 John 2:16.)
3. That they walk humbly before their God.
4. That the leaders stand firm in the Word of God.

III. Deception
Pray:

1. That the leaders not be led astray nor into error by false doctrine(s) and false prophets. (See Matt. 24:24.)

2. That they not be enamored by signs and wonders from the enemy.

3. That the leaders be kept from error and know the truth so it will keep them free. (See John 8:32.)

4. That the leaders hide the Word in their hearts.

5. That they not walk in hypocrisy or be bound by religious spirits.

6. That they pursue the love of truth.

7. That the leaders not be deceived by an antichrist, antichurch or unholy spirit that operates in signs and wonders.

IV. Enemies

Pray:

1. Against principalities, powers, rulers of darkness and spiritual wickedness in high places that come against the leaders, their families, ministries and the nations they are in. (See Eph. 6:12.)

2. Against occult activity—curses, witchcraft, divination, sorcery—in this manner:

   a. Bind the strongman. (See Ps. 149; Matt. 12:29; 16:19.)

   b. Destroy the works of the enemy. (See prayer in "The Name of Jesus: Our Authority," chapter 8.) For this purpose, Jesus was manifested. (See 1 John 3:8.)

   c. Ask God to foil the signs of the false prophets and make fools of the diviners. (See Isa. 44:25.)

   d. Send back double the deeds of destruction as they were sent to the leaders, their families and their properties. (See Rev. 18:6.)

   e. Ask that the enemies fall into their own traps while the leaders walk by safely. (See Ps. 141:9,10.)

   f. Ask the Lord to avenge His people. (See Pss. 35; 37.)

   g. Ask for God's most perfect will to be accomplished in the leaders.

h. Ask God to restore that which the enemy tried to steal, kill and destroy.

i. Ask that the Holy Spirit fill the leaders with the fruit of the Spirit and minister restoration. (See Isa. 61; Matt. 12:43-45; Gal. 5:22.)

Definitions:

Occult: Literally "hidden." Hidden from the eyes or understanding; invisible; secret; unknown; undiscovered; undetected.

Curse: To utter a wish of evil against one; to invoke evil upon; to call for mischief or injury to fall upon; to execrate; to injure; to subject to evil; to vex, harass or torment with great calamities.

Witchcraft: The practice of witches; sorcery; enchantment; unnatural power; intercourse with the devil.

Divination: The act of divining; foretelling future events, or discovering things secret or obscure by the aid of superior beings, or by other than human means.

Sorcery: Magic; enchantment; witchcraft; divination by assistance or supposed assistance of evil spirits, or the power of commanding evil spirits.

THURSDAY PRAYER
Safety, Protection, Release

From Fear

Father, I come before You in the name of Jesus, our Great High Priest who is touched with the feelings of our infirmities. Father, I'm interceding for (names). Thank You for hearing and answering my prayer. (See Heb. 4:15.)

The Lord lives, and blessed be their rock. And exalted be the God of salvation, for You execute vengeance for them, and subdue peoples under them. You deliver (names) from their enemies; surely You lift them above those who rise up against them; You rescue them from the violent man. Therefore, they will give thanks to You among the nations, O Lord, and will sing praises to Your name. For You give great deliverance to them, and show loving-kindness to Your anointed, and their descendants forever. (See Ps. 18:46-50.)

Father, because (names) listen to You and Your wisdom, they shall live securely, and shall be at ease from the dread of evil. Because they have made the Lord their refuge, even the Most High their dwelling place, no evil will befall them, nor will any plague come near their tent. (See Prov. 1:33; Ps. 91:9,10.)

Father, I pray for (names) to take up the full armor of God that they may be able to resist in the evil day, and that they, having done everything, may stand firm, having girded their loins with truth, and having put on the breastplate of righteousness, and having shod their feet with the preparation of the gospel of peace. In addition to all, may they take up the shield of faith with which they will be able to extinguish all the flaming missiles of the evil one, and taking the helmet of salvation, and the sword of the Spirit, which is the Word of God, with all prayer and petition, may they pray at all times in the Spirit, and with this in view, be on the alert with all perseverance and petition for all the saints. (See Eph. 6:13-18.)

Thank You, Lord, that in righteousness (names) will be established; they will be far from oppression, for they will not fear; and from terror, for it will not come near them. And if anyone fiercely assails them it will not be from You, for whoever assails them will fall because of them. Father, You declared that no weapon formed against them shall prosper, and every tongue that accuses them in judgment they will condemn. For this is the heritage of Your servants, and their vindication is from You. (See Isa. 54:14,15,17.)

For You did not give (names) a spirit of timidity, but You have given them a spirit of power and of love and of a calm and well-balanced mind and discipline and self-control. (See 2 Tim. 1:7.)

I pray, Father, that (names) will be strong and coura-geous, that they not tremble or be dismayed, for You are with them wherever they go. For greater is He who is in them than he who is in the world. (See Josh. 1:9; 1 John 4:4.)

Thank You, Father, that the angel of the Lord encamps around (names) because they fear You, and he rescues them. You are their confidence, and will keep their feet from being caught. (See Ps. 34:7; Prov. 3:26.)

Thank You, Father, that You have given them authori-ty through Jesus to tread upon serpents and scorpions, and over all the power of the enemy, and nothing shall injure them. (See Luke 10:19.)

From Enemies

O, Father, keep (names) as the apple of Your eye; hide them in the shadow of Your wings, from the wicked who despoil them, from their deadly enemies, who surround them. (See Ps. 17:8,9.)

Father, contend with those who contend with (names); fight against those who fight against them. For their eyes are toward You, O God, the Lord; in You they take refuge; do not leave them defenseless. Keep them from the jaws of the traps which have been set for them, and from the snares of those who do iniquity. Let the wicked fall into their own nets, while (names) pass by safely. (See Pss. 35:1; 141:8-10.)

From Temptation

Father, I ask that You not lead Your servants into temptation, but deliver them from evil. (See Matt. 6:13.)

I thank You, Father, that no temptation has overtaken (names) but such as is common to man; for You are faithful, and will not allow them to be tempted beyond what they are able, but with the temptation, You will provide the way of escape also, that they may be able to endure it. (See 1 Cor. 10:13.)

Thank You, Father, that You give greater grace. Therefore, it says, "God is opposed to the proud, but gives grace to the humble." I pray, Father, that (names) submit to You, that they may resist the devil and he will flee from them. I pray they will draw near to You, and You will draw near to them. I pray that (names) cleanse their hands, and purify their hearts, in order that they will not be double minded. (See Jas. 4:6-8.)

Father, since Jesus, Himself, was tempted in that which He suffered, He is able to come to the aid of those who are tempted. Since we do not have a High Priest who cannot sympathize with our weaknesses—but one who was tempted in all things as we are, yet without sin—I pray that (names) will therefore draw near with confidence to the throne of grace, that they may receive mercy and find grace to help in time of need. (See Heb. 4:14-16.)

From Deception

I pray, Father, that (names) will beware of the false prophets, who come to them in sheep's clothing, but inwardly are ravenous wolves. I pray (names) will know and recognize them by their fruits. For every good tree bears good fruit, but the rotten tree bears bad fruit. (See Matt. 7:15-17.)

Father, may (names) see to it that no one misleads them, for Jesus said that many will come in His name, saying, "I am the Christ," and will mislead many. For false Christs and false prophets will arise and will show great signs and wonders, so as to mislead, if possible, even the elect. (See Matt. 24:4,5,24.)

Father, I pray (names) will not believe every spirit, but will test the spirits to see whether they are from You, because many false prophets have gone out into the world. By this they will know the Spirit of God: every spirit that confesses that Jesus Christ has come in the flesh is from God; and every spirit that does not confess Jesus is not from God; and this is the spirit of the antichrist, of which we have heard that it is coming, and now it is already in the world. (See 1 John 4:1-3.)

I pray, Father, that (names) not be taken captive through philosophy and empty deception, according to the tradition of men, according to the elementary principles of the world, rather than according to Christ. For in Him they have been made complete, and He (Christ) is the overall rule and authority. (See Col. 2:8.)

From Overcoming Powers of Darkness

Thank You, Father, You have given to us the keys to the kingdom of heaven, and whatever we bind on earth, shall be bound in heaven, and whatever we loose on earth shall be loosed in heaven. (See Matt. 16:19.)

Father, in Jesus' name, I bind and break off of (names) and their families and ministries and all things that concern them: all principalities, powers, rulers of darkness of this world, and spiritual wickedness in high places, all occult activity—curses, witchcraft, divination and sorcery. I destroy the works of the enemy over them, and come against any soul power or emotional ties that do not glorify You.

Father, I ask that You forgive (names) for the sins of their youth, all vows, judgments, agreements with lies, and the sins and iniquities of their fathers, back through all generations, including all idle, negative words and curses over them in Jesus' name.

I loose (names) and their families and those with them in the ministry, and all things that concern them into the glorious liberty of the children of God, in the precious name of Jesus. If therefore the Son shall make them free, they shall be free indeed.

(Study references: Gen. 26:28; Exod. 20:5,6; 34:7,15; Num. 30:2; Deut. 5:9,10; 23:21; 24:16; Ps. 25:7; Prov. 6:16-19; 12:13,14; 13:2,3; Eccles. 5:4-7; Isa. 28:15,18; Jer. 31:19; 32:18; Dan. 9:4-20; Hos. 10:4; Luke 6:37,38; John 8:36; Rom. 2:1-6; Eph. 6:12,17; 2 Thess. 2:10-12; Heb. 3:19; 4:11; Jas. 4:11,12; 1 John 1:7,9.)

Thank You, Father, (names) have overcome the enemy because of the blood of the Lamb, and because of the word of their testimony, and they do not love their lives even to death. (See Rev. 12:11.)

Thank You, Father, that (names) have redemption through Jesus' blood, the forgiveness of their trespasses, according to the riches of Your grace. (See Eph. 1:7.)

Thank You, Father, as the redeemed of the Lord, (names) say so, whom Jesus has redeemed from the hand of the adversary. (See Ps. 107:2.)

Much more, then, having now been justified by Jesus' blood, (names) shall be saved from wrath through Him. For if while they were enemies they were reconciled to You through the death of Your Son, Jesus, much more, having been reconciled, they shall be saved by His life. (See Rom. 5:9,10.)

Thank You, Father, that You made Jesus, who knew no sin to be sin on (name)'s behalf, that they might become the righteousness of God in Him. Therefore, Jesus also, that He might sanctify them through His own blood, suffered outside the gate. (See 2 Cor. 5:21; Heb. 13:12.)

I pray, Father, that there be no strange god among (names), and that they not worship any foreign god. I pray they will not be bound together with unbelievers; for what partnership have righteousness and lawlessness, or what fellowship has light with darkness. (See Ps. 81:9; 2 Cor. 6:14.)

Thank You, Father, that (names) are a temple of God, and the Spirit of God dwells in them. (See 1 Cor. 3:16.)

FRIDAY
Priorities

I. Finances
Pray:

1. The Lord will cause the leaders to abound in prosperity—spirit, soul and body.
2. Thank Him for providing for all needs:
   a. Personal
   b. Family
   c. Ministry
3. Ask Him to stir up supporters for the ministry who will be obedient in giving; bless/prosper them for their giving.
4. For the ministry to have favor in the eyes of supporters.
5. Thank God that He will rebuke the devourer when he comes to steal what rightly belongs to the ministry of the leaders you pray for.

II. Priorities
Pray:

1. For discernment to get priorities in order.
2. For leaders to be open to God's changes and adjustments.
3. For leaders to learn to be wise stewards of time; become disciplined.
4. For leaders' relationship with God to always remain top priority.

III. Blessings
Pray:

1. Ask God to bless them because they give tithes and offerings and are cheerful givers.
2. Thank God that His Word says He delights to bless His servants; ask Him to bless the leaders you pray for.
3. Thank God for continuing to bless your leaders even into old age as they serve in His kingdom.

FRIDAY PRAYER

Finances

Father, in Jesus name, I pray for (names). I praise You for Your faithfulness to Your Word. Father, I pray that Your Word will be breathed upon by Your Holy Spirit, in order that it will accomplish the purposes of Your heart that You've sent it to do.

O, Father, You love (names) who love You, and I pray they will diligently seek You in order to find You. For riches and honor are with You, enduring wealth and righteousness. (See Prov. 8:17,18.)

Father, You cause those who love You to inherit substance, and You will fill their treasuries. (See Prov. 8:21.)

Thank You, Father, because the Lord is (name)'s Shepherd; they shall not want. And thank You, Father, because of the grace of our Lord Jesus Christ, that even though He was rich, yet for their sakes, He became poor, that they through His poverty might become rich. (See Ps. 23:1; 2 Cor. 8:9.)

Father, I pray (names) will have pity on the poor, for they that have pity on the poor lend to You, and that which they have given will You pay them again. (See Prov. 19:17.)

Father, I pray that as (names) give, it will be given to them; good measure, pressed down, shaken together, running over, it will pour into their laps. For whatever measure they deal out to others, it will be dealt to them in return. (See Luke 6:38.)

So, Father, I pray they sow bountifully in order to reap bountifully. May they give as they have purposed in their hearts, not grudgingly or under compulsion, for You love a cheerful giver. And You are able to make all grace abound to (names), that always having all sufficiency in everything, they may have an abundance for every good deed. As it is written, "He scattered abroad, He gave to the poor, His righteousness abides forever." Thank You, Father, You who supply seed to the sower and bread for food, will supply and multiply (name)'s seed for sowing and increase the harvest of their righteousness; You will enrich them in everything for all liberality. (See 2 Cor. 9:6-11a.)

Thank You, Father, that Jesus came that (names) might have life, and that they might have it more abundantly. (See John 10:10b.)

Prosperity

The Lord be magnified, who delights in the prosperity of His servants. (See Ps. 35:27b.)

Father, I pray (names) will not walk in the counsel of the wicked, nor stand in the path of sinners, nor sit in the seat of scoffers. But that their delight be in the law of the Lord, and in Your law they meditate day and night. I pray (names) be like trees firmly planted by the streams of water, which yield their fruit in season, their leaves do not wither; and in whatever they do, they prosper. (See Ps. 1:1-3.)

I pray, Father, that this book of the law shall not depart from their mouths, but (names) shall meditate on it day and night, so that they may be careful to do according to all that is written in it; for then they will make their way prosperous, and then, they will deal wisely and have good success. (See Josh. 1:8.)

Father, I pray that (names) will listen to Your commandments, and will diligently obey You, observing carefully to do all Your commandments which You have commanded them, so that they may be blessed in all that they put their hands to, in the land which You've given to them, both in the city, and in the country, abounding in all prosperity. (See Deut. 28:1-3,8,11.)

Father, I pray that in all respects, (names) may prosper and be in good health, even as their souls prosper. (See 3 John 2.)

Tithing

I pray that (names) honor You with their capital and sufficiency from righteous labors, and with the first fruits of all their income, in order that their storage places may be filled with plenty, and their vats be overflowing with new wine. (See Prov. 3:9,10.)

Father, I pray (names) will bring the whole tithe into the storehouse, so that there may be food in Your house. I pray that they will test You now in this matter to see if You will not open for them the windows of heaven, and pour out for (names) a blessing until there is no more need or room. Then You will rebuke the devourer for them, so that he may not destroy the fruits of the ground; nor will their vine in the field cast its fruit. And all will call (names) blessed, for they shall be a delightful land. (See Mal. 3:10-12.)

Needs and Priorities

Father, You did not spare Your own Son, Jesus, but delivered Him up for us all. How then will You not also with Him freely give (names) all things? (See Rom. 8:32.)

Thank You, Father, You regard the prayer of the destitute, and will not despise their prayer. (See Ps. 102:17.)

Father, I pray that (names) will seek first Your kingdom and Your righteousness, in order that all these things may be added to them. (See Matt. 6:33.)

I pray they will be anxious for nothing, but in everything by prayer and supplication with thanksgiving, (names) will let their requests be made known to You. And Your peace, which surpasses all comprehension, shall guard their hearts and minds in Christ Jesus. (See Phil. 4:6,7.)

Father, I pray that (names) may fear You according to Your Word; for there is no want to them who fear You. The young lions do lack and suffer hunger, but they who seek You will not be in want of any good thing. (See Ps. 34:9,10.)

Thank You, Father, for supplying every need of (names) according to Your riches in glory in Christ Jesus. (See Phil. 4:19.)

For every good thing bestowed and every perfect gift is from above, coming down from You, Father of lights, with whom there is no variation, or shifting shadow. (See Jas. 1:17.)

Blessings

I bless You, Lord, for You daily load (names) with bene-fits. You are the God of their salvation. I bless You, Lord. (See Ps. 68:19.)

Father, Your blessing makes (names) rich, and You add no sorrow with it. (See Prov. 10:22.)

Father, I pray that because (names) are generous, they will be blessed. (See Prov. 22:9.)

I pray they be blessed to find wisdom, and gain understanding. For long life is in her right hand, and in her left hand are riches and honor. She is a tree of life to those who take hold of her, and happy are (names) who hold her fast. (See Prov. 3:13,16,18.)

For You, Lord, give grace and glory; no good thing will You withhold from (names) because they walk uprightly. O Lord of hosts, how blessed they are because they trust in You. (See Ps. 84:11,12.)

I pray that (names) delight themselves in You, Lord, for You will give them the desires of their hearts. You know their days, and their inheritance will be forever. They will not be ashamed in the time of evil, and in the days of famine they will have abundance. (See Ps. 37:4,18,19.)

SATURDAY
Family

I. Family—General
Pray:

1. For unity and understanding.
2. For no resentment when sacrifice is required.
3. For sharing the vision of ministry; being active in it.
4. For sharing in prayer and devotions as family.
5. For each to operate in God-given gifts and talents.
6. For a hospitable home, open to others.
7. For all to be fervent in spirit, serving the Lord.

II. Husband and Wife
Pray:

1. To meet emotional needs of the family.
2. To be sensitive to family needs.
3. To communicate well with each family member.
4. To be a sympathetic listener to each family member.
5. For husband to lead family in devotions and prayer on a regular basis.
6. To spend quality time with family—both leisure time and spiritual time.
7. To recognize they are a team, made to encourage and help one another with loyalty.
8. To complement and complete one another.
9. To discern each other's needs: emotional, physical, material and spiritual.
10. To have the fruit of the Spirit in their lives.
11. To have fulfillment of their own spiritual relationship and hear God's voice.
12. To have strength to overcome pressures and stress.
13. To resist living up to other people's expectations, released to be a unique person, and a unique couple.
14. For each to find their individual niche in the kingdom of God.

III. Children
Pray:

1. That the children be trained in reverential fear of the Lord.
2. That the children show love, patience, understanding and loyalty toward family and ministry.
3. That the children choose righteous friends at school, home, work and in their social lives.
4. For good relationships to prevail among the children in the family.
5. That the children be involved in parents' ministry at

the level where God has called them to participate.

6. That there be no resentment or competition among family members.
7. That the children be obedient and righteous.
8. That the children be flexible, able to adapt to change, moving and culture.
9. That the children be free from expectations put on them by themselves or others that are not in line with God's will.
10. That the children be able to hear God's voice individually.

SATURDAY PRAYER

Family—General

Father, in Jesus' name, I pray for (names). May they reign in life today through our Lord Jesus Christ, having received the abundance of grace and the gift of righteousness. For Your eyes are toward the righteous, and Your ears are open to their cry. (See Rom. 5:17; Ps. 34:15.)

Thank You, Father, that because (names) have believed in the Lord Jesus, they and their household shall be saved. Thank You, that as for (names) and their house, they will serve the Lord. (See Acts 16:31; Josh. 24:15.)

I pray that (names) might be filled with the knowledge of Your will in all wisdom and spiritual understanding, in order that they might walk worthy of You, unto all pleasing, being fruitful in every good work, and increasing in the knowledge of God, that they might be strengthened with all might, according to Your glorious power, unto all patience and long-suffering with joyfulness. (See Col. 1:9-11.)

Father, I pray that (names) will not be anxious, saying, "What shall we eat?" or "What shall we drink?" or "With what shall we clothe ourselves?" For all these things the Gentiles eagerly seek. For You know, Heavenly Father, that they need all these things. I pray they will seek first Your kingdom and Your righteousness, and all these things shall be added to them. I pray they will not be anxious for tomorrow, for tomorrow will care for itself. (See Matt. 6:31-34.)

Thank You, Father, that Your eye is on (names) because they fear You; they hope in Your loving-kindness, to deliver their souls from death, and to keep them alive in famine. (See Ps. 33:18,19.)

Father, by wisdom may (name)'s house be built, and by understanding may it be established. By knowledge may their rooms be filled with all precious and pleasant riches. The curse of the Lord is on the house of the wicked, but You bless the dwelling of (names), the righteous. (See Prov. 24:3,4; 3:33.)

Because they fear You, Father, You will instruct (names) in the way they should choose, and their souls will abide in prosperity, and their descendants will inherit the land. Your secret counsel and sweet, satisfying companionship is for those who fear You, and You will make (names) to know Your covenant, and reveal to them its deep, inner meaning. Their eyes are continually toward You, for You will pluck their feet out of the net. All Your paths are loving-kindness and truth to them, because (names) keep Your covenant and Your testimonies. Redeem them, Father, out of all their troubles. (See Ps. 25:12-15,10,22.)

Children

Thank You, Father, that (name)'s children are a gift and a heritage from You, and the fruit of the womb is their reward from You. The children of their youth are like arrows in the hand of a warrior. How blessed they are to have their quiver full of them; they shall not be ashamed when they speak with their enemies in the gate. (See Ps. 127:3-5.)

You said, Father, that even the captives of the mighty man will be taken away, and the prey of the tyrant will be rescued. You will contend with the ones who contend with (names), and You will save their children. (See Isa. 49:25.)

I pray, Father, they will train up their children in the

way they should go, so that even when their children are old, they will not depart from it. (See Prov. 22:6.)

Father, thank You that all of (name)'s children will be taught by You, and the peace and well-being of their children will be great. (See Isa. 54:13.)

I pray that (name)'s children be obedient to their parents in all things, for this is well pleasing to You; that they honor their father and their mother, which is the first commandment with a promise, that it may be well with them; and that they may live long on the earth. (See Col. 3:20; Eph. 6:1-3.)

I ask, Father, that You give to (name)'s children the tongue of disciples, that they may know how to sustain the weary one with a word, and awaken their ear to listen as a disciple, and not be disobedient nor rebellious. For You will help them; therefore, they will not be ashamed, confounded, or turned backward. (See Isa. 50:4,5,7.)

I pray that all may desire to know how to follow (name)'s example, because their children do not act in an undisciplined manner among others. (See 2 Thess. 3:7.)

I pray that the fathers do not provoke their children to anger, but bring them up in the discipline and instruction of the Lord. I pray that the fathers not exasperate them, in order that they not lose heart. (See Eph. 6:4; Col. 3:21.)

Father, I pray that (name)'s children hearken and listen to You, that You may teach them the fear of the Lord. May their children keep their tongues from evil, and their lips from speaking deceit. May they depart from evil, and do good. May these children seek peace, and pursue it, in order that they may have life and length of days, and that they may see good. (See Ps. 34:11-14.)

And, Father, I pray (name)'s offspring shall be known among the nations, and their descendants among the peoples, that all who see them in their prosperity will recognize and acknowledge they are the people whom You have blessed. (See Isa. 61:9.)

Husband

Father, so that (names) may be above reproach, I pray that they provide for their own, especially for those of their own household, that they do not deny the faith, and be worse than an unbeliever. (See 1 Tim. 5:7,8.)

Father, I pray that just as Christ was faithful as a Son over His house, so also will (names) be faithful over their house. (See Heb. 3:6.)

I pray, Father, that they each may know how to possess their own vessels in sanctification and honor, and not in lustful passion, like the Gentiles, who do not know God. (See 1 Thess. 4:4,5.)

I pray that the husband will live with his wife in an understanding way, as with a weaker vessel, since she is a woman, and grant her honor as a fellow-heir of the grace of life, so that their prayers be not hindered. (See 1 Pet. 3:7.)

Wife

Thank You, Father, that You have made a suitable helper for (names). (See Gen. 2:18.)

I pray the heart of her husband trusts in her, and that he will have no lack of gain. I pray that she will do him good, and not evil, all the days of her life, and that he will be known in the gates when he sits among the elders of the land. (See Prov. 31:11,12,23.)

I pray that strength and dignity are her clothing, and that she smiles at the future. I pray she opens her mouth in wisdom, and the teaching of kindness is on her tongue. I pray that she looks well to the ways of her household, and does not eat the bread of idleness. (See Prov. 31:25-27.)

Couple

I pray their way of life be free from the love of money, being content with what they have, for You said You would never desert them, nor will You ever forsake them, because godliness with contentment is great gain. (See Heb. 13:5; 1 Tim. 6:6.)

I pray they always give a soft, gentle answer to turn away wrath, because grievous, harsh words stir up anger. (See Prov. 15:1.)

I pray that (name)'s love will be without hypocrisy. I pray they will abhor what is evil and cling to what is good. I pray they will be devoted to one another in brotherly love; giving preference to one another in honor; not lagging behind in diligence; fervent in spirit; serving the Lord; rejoicing in hope; persevering in tribulation; devoted to prayer; contributing to the needs of the saints; practicing hospitality. (See Rom. 12:9-13.)

Family

And so, Father, as those who have been chosen of God, holy and beloved, I pray that (names) put on a heart of compassion, kindness, humility, gentleness and patience; bearing with one another, and forgiving each other, whoever has a complaint against anyone, just as You forgave them, so also will they. And beyond all these, that they put on love, which is the perfect bond of unity. And I pray they let the peace of Christ rule in their hearts, to which indeed they were called in one body, and be thankful. (See Col. 3:12-15.)

As for You, Father, this is Your covenant or league with (names): Your Spirit who is upon them and who writes the law of God inwardly in their hearts, and Your words which You have put in their mouths, shall not depart out of their mouths, or out of the mouths of their children, or out of the mouths of their children's children from henceforth, and forever. (See Isa. 59:21.)

Now that you have a clear understanding of how to pray, allow God to birth His purposes and plans through you for the wounded and dying world that surrounds you. As you make prayer a priority, you will be changed and God will use you to change your world.

Glossary

Angels: Spirit beings created to serve and minister to God (see Heb. 1:7).

Anointing: The presence, power and ministry of the Holy Spirit.

Assignment: A specified task or amount of work assigned or undertaken as if assigned by authority; trust and responsibility for completion of a task.

Body of Christ: All born-again believers in Jesus Christ; embodies all denominations who believe Jesus Christ is God.

Confession: To speak forth acknowledgment of a belief; to disclose one's faults.

Curse: To utter evil against one; to invoke evil upon; to call for mischief or injury to fall upon; to execrate; to injure; to subject to evil; to vex, harass or torment with great calamities.

Deliverance: Setting a person or area free from demonic bondage.

Demons: Created spirit beings who were thrown out of heaven by God for rebelling against Him and declaring allegiance to Satan; evil spirits.

Divination: The practice that seeks to foresee or foretell future events or discover hidden knowledge by the aid of supernatural powers.

Holy of Holies: The innermost section of the Tabernacle and the Temple of God. The high priest went into the Holy of Holies only once a year, where he met with God and offered a blood sacrifice for the atonement of the people's sins.

Iniquity: Gross injustice; wickedness.

Intercession: Prayer petition or entreaty in favor of another. Through prayer this is an extension of Jesus' act of intercession when He died on the cross in man's behalf.

Occult: Literally "hidden." Hidden from the eyes of our understanding; invisible; secret; unknown; undiscovered; undetected.

Petition: An earnest request of God.

Plead the blood of Jesus: To remind oneself and Satan that he has no authority over the person for whom you are praying, because of the blood sacrifice made by Jesus Christ.

Praise (Godward): To express a favorable judgment of God; to commend, speak and attribute approval of God's character or actions (to Him).

Praying in the Spirit: Praying in a language unknown to one's own mind.

Repentance: To turn away from sin and sinning and amend one's lifestyle to please God.

Satan: The created cherub (angelic being) called Lucifer who was thrown out of heaven by God for rebelling against God and trying to steal His glory. The father of lies.

Sin: Anything in the creature which does not express, or is contrary to, the holy character of the Creator.

Sorcery: Magic; enchantment; witchcraft; divination by assistance or supposed assistance of evil spirits; the power of commanding evil spirits.

Spiritual discernment: The gift of the Holy Spirit given to Christians to distinguish between what is of God and what is evil.

Stronghold: A fortified place. A place of security or survival; specifically dominated by a particular group or characteristic. A person's thought life can have many strongholds.

Tithe: A tenth part of something paid as a voluntary contribution to God as an acknowledgment that all you have comes from and belongs to Him (see Mal. 3:10).

Witchcraft: The use of sorcery or magic; communication with the devil or with a familiar spirit; enchantment; unnatural power.

Recommended Reading

Alves, Elizabeth. *Praying with Purpose: Families*. Bulverde, Tex.: Canopy Press, 1996.

Barton, Dave. *America: To Pray or Not to Pray?* Aledo, Tex.: Wallbuilder Press, 1988.

Bernal, Dick. *Storming Hell's Brazen Gates*. San Jose, Calif.: Jubilee Christian Center, 1988.

Bloesch, Donald G. *The Struggle of Prayer*. Colorado Springs: Helmer & Howard, 1988.

Boschman, LaMar. *The Rebirth of Music*. Bedford, Tex.: Revival Press, 1980.

Bounds, E. M. *Power Through Prayer*. Grand Rapids: Zondervan Publishing House, 1987.

——. *The Best of E. M. Bounds on Prayer*. Grand Rapids: Baker Book House, 1987.

Bright, Bill. *Seven Basic Steps to Successful Fasting and Prayer*. Orlando: New Life Publications, 1995.

Bryant, David. *Concerts of Prayer*. Rev. ed. Ventura, Calif.: Regal Books, 1988.

Chatham, R. D. *Fasting: A Biblical-Historical Study*. Southfield, N.J.: Bridge, 1987.

Cho, Paul Yonggi. *Prayer: Key to Revival*. Dallas, Tex.: Word Books, 1984.

Christenson, Evelyn. *What Happens When Women Pray*. Wheaton, Ill.: Victor Books, 1975.

Daugherty, Billy Joe. *Principles of Prayer*. Victory Christian Center, 7700 South Louis Ave., Tulsa, Okla. 7431-7700. 1996.

Dawson, John. *Taking Our Cities for God*. Lake Mary, Fla.: Creation House, 1989.

Dawson, Joy. *Intimate Friendship with God*. Grand Rapids: Chosen Books, 1986.

Deere, Jack. *Surprised by the Power of the Spirit*. Grand Rapids: Zondervan Publishing, 1993.

Eastman, Dick. *The Hour That Changes the World*. Grand Rapids: Baker Book House, 1978.

——. *The Jericho Hour*. Orlando, Fla.: Creation House, 1994.

——. *Love on Its Knees*. Grand Rapids: Chosen Books, 1989.

——. *No Easy Road*. Grand Rapids: Baker Book House, 1978.

Eastman, Dick and Jack Hayford. *Living and Praying in Jesus' Name*. Wheaton, Ill.: Tyndale House, 1988.

Edward, Gene. *A Tale of Three Kings*. Wheaton, Ill.: Tyndale House, 1992.

Femrite, Barbara. *Praying with Purpose: Unreached Peoples*. Bulverde, Tex.: Canopy Press, 1997.

Frangipane, Francis. *Holiness, Truth and the Presence of God*. Cedar Rapids, Ia.: Advancing Church Publications, 1986.

——. *House of the Lord*. Lake Mary, Fla.: Creation House, 1991.

——. *The Three Battlegrounds*. Cedar, Ia.: Arrow Publishing, 1989.

Goll, Jim W. *The Lost Art of Intercession*. Revival Press, P.O. Box 310, Shippensburg, Pa. 17257-0310. 1997.

Greenwald, Gary. *Seductions Exposed*. Santa Ana, Calif.: Eagle's Nest Publications, 1988.

Grubb, Norman. *Rees Howells, Intercessor*, 3rd ed. Fort Washington, Pa.: Christian Literature Crusade, 1983.

Gurnall, William. *The Christian in Complete Armour*. Lindale, Tex.: Banner of Truth Trust, 1991.

Guyon, Jeanne. *Experiencing the Depths of Jesus Christ*. Gardiner, Me.: Christian Books, 1981.

Haggard, Ted and Jack Hayford. *Loving Your City into the Kingdom*. Ventura, Calif: Regal Books, 1997.

Harper, Michael. *Spiritual Warfare*. Plainfield, N.J.: Logos International, 1970.

Harrison House. *Prayers That Avail Much*. Tulsa, Okla., 1989.

Hawthorne, Steve and Graham Kendrick. *Prayerwalking*. Orlando, Fla.: Creation House, 1993.

Hayford, Jack W. *Prayer Is Invading the Impossible*. New York: Ballantine Books, 1983.

Jacobs, Cindy. *Possessing the Gates of the Enemy*. Grand Rapids: Chosen Books, 1991.

——. *The Voice of God*. Ventura, Calif.: Regal Books, 1995.

Kinnaman, Gary. *Overcoming the Dominion of Darkness*. Grand Rapids: Chosen Books, 1990.

Law, Terry. *The Power of Praise and Worship*. Tulsa, Okla.: Victory House, Inc., 1985.

Lea, Larry. *Could You Not Tarry One Hour?* Lake Mary, Fla.: Creation House, 1987.

LeSourd, Leonard E. *Touching the Heart of God*. Grand Rapids: Chosen Books, 1990.

Lindsay, Gordon. *Prayer That Moves Mountains*. Rev. Dallas, Tex.: Christ For The Nations, 1994.

Marshall, Catherine. *Adventures in Prayer*. Grand Rapids: Revell, 1966.

Matthews, R. Arthur. *Born for Battle*. Robesonia, Pa.: OMF Books, 1978.

Maxwell, John. *The Pastor's Prayer Partners*. Bonita, Calif.: Injoy Ministries, 1989.

Mills, Dick. *He Spoke and I Was Strengthened.* San Jacinto, Calif.: Dick Mills Ministries, 1991.

Moody, Dwight. *Prevailing Prayer.* Chicago: Moody Press, 1980.

Mueller, George. *Answers to Prayer.* Chicago: Moody Press, 1984.

Murray, Andrew. *The Believer's School of Prayer.* Bloomington, Minn.: Bethany, 1998.

———. *The Ministry of Intercessory Prayer.* Bloomington, Minn.: Bethany, 1998.

———. *With Christ in the School of Prayer.* Reprint. Grand Rapids: Zondervan, 1983 (first published in 1885).

Nee, Watchman. *The Release of the Spirit.* Cloverdale, Ind.: Sure Foundation Publishers, 1965.

———. *Spiritual Authority.* Richmond, Va.: Christian Fellowship Publisher, 1972.

Peretti, Frank E. *This Present Darkness.* Westchester, Ill.: Crossway Books, 1986.

Sampson, Steve. *You Can Hear the Voice of God.* Kent, England: Sovereign World, 1993.

Sandford, John and Paula. *The Elijah Task.* Tulsa, Okla.: Victory House, Inc., 1986.

Shaw, Gwen. *God's End-Time Battle-Plan.* Jasper, Ark.: Engeltal Press, 1984.

Sheets, Dutch. *Intercessory Prayer.* Ventura, Calif.: Regal Books, 1996.

Sherman, Dean. *Spiritual Warfare for Every Christian.* Seattle, Wash.: Frontline Communications, 1990.

Sherrer, Quin. *How to Pray for Your Family and Friends.* Ann Arbor, Mich.: Servant Publications, 1990.

———. *How to Pray for Your Children.* Lynnwood, Wash.: Aglow Publications, 1986.

———. *Miracles Happen When You Pray.* Grand Rapids: Zondervan Publishing House, 1997.

———. *Prayers Women Pray.* Ann Arbor, Mich.: Servant Publications, 1998.

Sherrer, Quin and Ruthanne Garlock. *A Woman's Guide to Spiritual Warfare.* Ann Arbor, Mich.: Servant Publications, 1991.

———. *How to Forgive Your Children.* Lynnwood, Wash.: Aglow Publications, 1989.

———. *The Spiritual Warrior's Prayer Guide.* Ann Arbor, Mich.: Servant Publications, 1992.

Shibley, David. *A Force in the Earth.* Lake Mary, Fla.: Creation House, 1989.

Shields, Paula. *Healing of the Soul.* Bulverde, Tex.: Intercessors International, 1991.

Sjöberg, Kjell. *Restoration: A Direction for Prayer.* New Wine Press, P.O. Box 17, Chichester, England PO206YB. 1995

———. *Winning the Prayer War.* Chichester, England: New Wine Press, 1991.

Smith, Alice. *Beyond the Veil.* Ventura, Calif.: Regal Books, 1997.

Ten Boom, Corrie. *Marching Orders for the End Battle.* Fort Washington, Pa.: Christian Literature Crusade, 1980.

Tippit, Sammy. *The Prayer Factor.* Chicago, Ill.: Moody Press, 1988.

Towe, Joy. *Praise Is.* Irving, Tex.: Triumphant Praise, 1979.

Towns, Elmer L. *Fasting for Spiritual Breakthrough.* Ventura, Calif.: Regal Books, 1991.

Wagner, C. Peter. *Breaking Strongholds in Your City.* Ventura, Calif.: Regal Books, 1993.

——. *Churches That Pray.* Ventura, Calif.: Regal Books, 1993.

——. *Confronting the Powers.* Ventura, Calif.: Regal Books, 1996.

——. *Engaging the Enemy.* ed. C. Peter Wagner, Ventura, Calif.: Regal Books, 1991.

——. *How to Have a Prayer Ministry.* Pasadena, Calif.: Charles E. Fuller Institute, 1990.

——. *Prayer Shield.* Ventura, Calif.: Regal Books, 1992.

——. *Praying with Power.* Ventura, Calif.: Regal Books, 1997.

——. *Warfare Prayer.* Ventura, Calif.: Regal Books, 1992.

——. *Your Spiritual Gifts Can Help Your Church Grow.* Ventura, Calif.: Regal Books, 1979.

Wagner, C. Peter and Douglas Pennoyer, eds. *Wrestling with Dark Angels.* Ventura, Calif.: Regal Books, 1990.

Wallis, Arthur. *God's Chosen Fast.* Fort Washington, Pa.: Christian Literature Crusade, 1968.

White, Thomas B. *The Believer's Guide to Spiritual Warfare.* Arbor, Mich.: Servant Publications, 1990.

Willhite, B. J. *Why Pray?* Lake Mary, Fla.: Creation House, 1988.

Wimber, John. *Teach Us to Pray.* Anaheim, Calif.: Vineyard Ministries International, 1986.

Also from Elizabeth Alves

Intercessors
Discover Your Prayer Power
Elizabeth Alves, Tommi Femrite,
Karen Kaufman
Paperback • ISBN 08307.26446

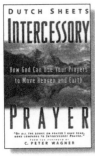